D1110598

Eat the Heat

Jonas Borssén

EAT THE HEAT

Ten Speed Press
Berkeley, California

🔟

Ten Speed Press
P.O. Box 7123
Berkeley, CA 94707

Cataloging-in-Publication Data on file with publisher.

Credits:

PHOTOGRAPHERS

Jonas Borssén, pages 8, 40, 45, 47, 57, 80, 94, 142, 145, 151.

Aldus Hulton Deutsch Collection, Vol. 3 page 6

Ingvar Eriksson, pages 90, 106, 108, 117, 121, 140, 147

Bjorn Lindberg, portrait on back cover and the photo which was used
for the hors d'oeuvres and dessert pages. Also pages 15, 28, 29,
48, 58, 60,62,67, 69, 70, 89, 92, 105, 127, 136, 139, 152

Boris Kaplja, National Ethnographic Museum, page 16.

Robert Lundin, page 26

Raimo Oravo, pages 9, 22, 25, 32, 33, 34, 38, 39, 41, 95.

Robert Reed, pages 11, 78, 113, 135, 154.

Lars Svanstrom, pages 46, 96

Arie de Zanger, pages 64.

ILLUSTRATIONS
copyright © **Rand McNally,** page 10

The Town Library in Lund, page 17

The New York Public Library Picture Collection, pages 18, 19, 55,
64, 65, 68, 84, 90, 123, 128, 130, 132, 137, 151, 153.

Robert Reed, pages 65, 72, 80, 83, 98, 102, 116, 118, 120, 145, 165

The University of Stockholm Library, pages 20, 23

Cover and graphic design by Robert Reed
Cover photo by Eduardo Fuss
Reproduction and painting by Falths & Co., Varnamo, Sweden, 1996.

Table of Contents

Where There's Smoke There's Chile!

There is a peculiar enjoyment experienced when eating spicy food, a positive, elated feeling as paradoxical as a sauna during the winter, or the taste of ice-cold beer at a sweltering summer barbecue. The sensation of this gastronomic explosion is both loved and feared. Tolerance varies from person to person, but those of us who have a taste for it just crave it more and more.

Hot food lovers are increasing in number all the time. In 1992, salsa and hot sauce sales easily surpassed those of America's beloved tomato ketchup; this "hot trend" is noticeable all over the world. In Sweden alone, the importation of fresh chiles has increased by one ton per year since the early 1900s. If the expression "you are what you eat" is true, then the Swedish national character is changing dramatically.

With the increasing popularity of the chile, a whole new world of flavors, colors, and consistencies is being discovered. Besides enhancing the taste buds, chiles help you appreciate more sophisticated types of food, provide insight into new methods of cooking, and inspire learning about the ingredients which accompany chiles.

In this book, the words "chile" or "chile pepper" are used to describe the fruit, vegetable, and seasoning. However, the word "chili" appears in some recipes, such as Chili Con Frijoles.

But what is a chile?

Chiles belongs to the Capsicum family, which is related to the tomato, tobacco plant, and potato.

Chiles, however, are not related to the pepper we know as the household pepper, *Piper nigrum*. The structure of the Capsicum family is best explained in Dave DeWitt's book, *The Whole Chile Pepper Book* (1990). Chiles, like dogs, come in all shapes and sizes, pedigrees and temperaments. Certain chiles, like the cayenne and the jalapeño, are as different as the boxer and the

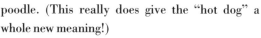

poodle. (This really does give the "hot dog" a whole new meaning!)

From a botanical point of view, the chile is a berry which is harvested and used as a vegetable and for seasoning. Its strength varies according to its size and shape; the smaller and longer and more pointed it is, the hotter it is. The larger and rounder ones are milder. Chile fruits also have a range of colors, from unripe green to a mature yellow, orange, red, brown, or lilac and many different shades in between. There are 150 to 200 different varieties of chiles and approximately 5,000 hybrids have been developed during the last 10 years. In this book I have chosen some of the most common. I hope that my interest in chiles will tempt you, and that you will become as enthusiastic about them as I am!

Southern Inspiration

Just as the truffle is a symbol of French gastronomy, the chile represents a new culinary era. Chile has always been one of the main ingredients in America's Southwest and Cajun cuisines. It maintains a prominent position in California and New Florida cooking, in turn inspiring cooks across the nation. They have discovered their American heritage and have captured and cultivated the nation's taste for trendy, fun food. Mouth-watering recipes are created using prime beef from Texas; Maine lobster; Wisconsin cheese; Louisiana crayfish; fine wines from the Napa Valley; Idaho potatoes; an abundance of vegetables, fruit, and fresh herbs from California; and, finally, chiles from New Mexico.

This spicy, cultural trend also fits well with our modern ideas about balancing protein, fat, carbohydrates, and fiber. Low fat content and maximum taste in vegetables, salsas, soups, and broths is today's gastronomical kick as we say goodbye to yesterday's heavy mayonnaise and cream sauce.

A happy cowboy with his October harvest by the Rio Grande in west Texas

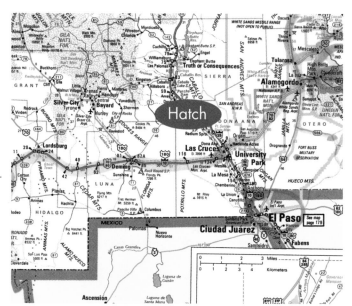

Hatch, which is the main chile plantation in Southern New Mexico

As a young cook in Sweden, I was trained in the new style of cooking—cooking which is full of character, imagination, and fun! The music of the Southern states enriched my food fantasy and made me curious to delve deeper into the customs of the American South. Joe "King" Carrasco's Tex-Mex sound and "Jalapeño con Big Red," had a good beat and were great for dancing music. Augie Meyers, the popular musician known for, among other things, The Sir Douglas Quintet and the Texas Tornadoes, showed me how to cook a Texas chili seasoned with jalapeño. On another occasion, Queen Ida offered me seafood gumbo and belted out "Hey Negresse" on the accordion. When I visited my friend, Jose, in Austin, Texas (whose father named his company eponymously, "Don Alfonso," which sells America's largest assortment of chiles), I was treated to freshly baked corn tortillas, chile rellenos, ceviche washed down with chile beer, and a large portion of Texan hospitality.

In 1987 I was enticed to Malmo in the Swedish South by the prospect of a partnership in the O'yes Bar and Restaurant. It was this particular year that O'yes was chosen as Restaurant of the Year by the Swedish trade press.

With its distinctive character, classical food, and cosmopolitan setting, O'yes became a landmark for the new food culture.

Even the music played a role in developing the menu: O'yes "Southern Nights" featured live appearances by Dr. John, Queen Ida, Lyle Lovett, and the Angela Strehli Band, and we cooks looked for creative ways to harmonize our food with the style of the music.

Once, we had guests from Cancún, in the Yucatán, who were cooks and loved beer. I made a wonderful trade. Their bill for the beer was exorbitant, but I exchanged it for a large assortment of chiles including the habanero, the strongest chile in the world, which they had with them. Chile was used as payment as early as during the time of the Incas, and it is an excellent exchange which still works today! The chiles proved to give me new inspiration and renewed pleasure in cooking.

Mark Miller, who is an anthropologist, restaurateur, and expert on chiles, explained to me that the introduction of spices throughout the centuries has played a great part in the use of chiles today. In Asia, for instance, chiles very quickly became an important part of the cookery because spices had always been used in abundance.

In Africa, paradise pepper or guinea pepper (which is related to ginger) was used before the arrival of chiles. Even in Europe chiles were welcomed with open arms because they were so inexpensive compared to black pepper. Chiles are also extremely easy to cultivate. In Mexico and Hungary, chiles and bell peppers are associated with the national identity. Today, chiles are on the cutting edge as enthusiasts from all over the world meet at chile festivals, trade fairs, and symposiums.

Fresh and Healthy with a Hot Bite

Live hot or die! Perhaps this is a rather drastic way of expressing it, but chiles can be described as a health food product: they have a lot of fiber and even more vitamins. They're also free from cholesterol and contain virtually no calories.

Can you go on a diet using chiles? Research suggests that it is possible. Scientists at the Polytechnic Institute in Oxford have established that ingested chile aids metabolism. Normally, the body's metabolism increases automatically after a meal, but when chile is added to the food, the effect is increased by an additional 25 percent.

Capsaicin gives the chile its hot taste and has a positive effect on the body. Capsaicin is a substance which is produced in the placenta of the pod; up to 90 percent of its strength is contained within these membranes. The seeds, however, have no strength of their own, but are influenced by their connection with the placenta.

Capsaicin is eighty times stronger than piperin, which is the substance that gives black pepper its strong taste. Not to worry, however. Scientists have proven that capsaicin is quite harmless to the stomach. Using volunteers, they injected chile pepper into the membranes of their stomachs, and with the help of fiber optics, concluded that the stomach was not in the least affected by it.

Chile has several delightful characteristics. When you eat spicy food, you will notice a feeling of well-being. Capsaicin stimulates the body's endorphins, which are similar to morphine and have the same pain-relieving and habit-forming effects. It is the same sort of experience as the athlete's so-called "jogger's high."

So before you take the first bite, don't forget to fasten your seatbelt—it's an exhilarating ride.

The discovery of vitamin C in chiles gave the Hungarian Professor Albert Szent-Gyorgyi the Nobel Prize in 1937. Today we know that chiles are highly nutritious and give a great vitamin kick with large amounts of both A and C. A chile contains more vitamin A than any other edible plant, and more than double the vitamin C of an orange.

Spanish sailors were probably unaware that they were protecting themselves from scurvy when they ate chiles pickled in vinegar during their travels to and from the New World. Today we know more about vitamin C and the role it plays in protecting the body against infections. Capsaicin has also been proven to have both a preventive and healing effect upon illnesses of the ear and nose.

Dr. Par Stjarne from the Karolinska Hospital in Stockholm has found out through research that chronic head colds with congestion and sneezing can be cured with the help of, guess what? Chiles! Capsaicinet in chiles makes the nerves in the mucus membranes resistant to infections; when consumption is repeated time and time again, the body's resistance to infection is increased for up to six months.

Perhaps the doctor of the future will write a prescription for a daily dose of cayenne to protect against the flu or suggest to the patient, "take two jalapeños and call me tomorrow."

The Peruvian expression "llevanta muertos" alludes to a type of chile which is incredibly hot, hot enough to "wake the dead." There are many myths, but the fact is that chiles are, and have been, a universal remedy in folk medicine. Even in the Swedish Pharmacopoeia, which described medicinal compositions, there is a prescription consisting of a mixture of alcohol and chile pepper which was used as a mouthwash and for gargling to cure tonsillitis, stomach problems, and flatulence.

In Jamaica, a drink is made from chiles to protect against tropical fever. The drink has also been used to treat malaria.

Another proven method that is still in use today is to powder the inside of one's socks with cayenne pepper—this warms up cold feet during the winter.

The German botanist, G. A. Schweinfurth, returned from Africa with the sensational news that the natives made a magical chile drink which gave one eternal youth. Schweinfurth died in 1925 so I suppose he never tasted this drink.

More believable are the reports regarding the chile's vascular dilatory effects. Capsaicin is used for external use in liniments, ointments, and warm cotton wool for rheumatism and pain in joints and muscles. Taken internally, capsaicinet helps to prevent heart and vascular diseases. Loss of appetite, nosebleeds, varicose veins, shingles, headaches, hangovers, and toothaches can also be cured or alleviated with chiles.

Above all else, chiles are appreciated for their tasty, strong flavor and for their versatility.

Pre-Columbian dishes with chile pepper ornamentation,
accompanied by birds and fishes, Cusco in Peru.

A Little History

Brother Chile

When you stand in your kitchen and mix a salsa seasoned with chiles, you may be interested to know that this tradition goes back at least ten thousand years. Chiles, along with corn, squash, and beans, were the first cultivated plants which could be used and eaten on the American continent and it was as important for the South and Middle American cultures as black pepper was for those of Asia and Europe.

The Incas in the Andes were dependent upon chiles and used them in all types of cooking. Chiles were also worshipped as one of the four brothers in their mythological story, "Brother Chile." The chile plant was regarded as sacred; eating it was cloaked in ritual. Most Incas were vegetarians, as meat and fish were upper-class luxuries. However, chiles were not only used in cooking, but also in folk medicine and as a means of payment. This was portrayed on textiles, ceramics, and obelisks.

From the Andes up to Mexico, chiles were also known as a drug. In Panama, the native tribes mixed chile with cocoa and tobacco. In Colombia it was mixed with cocaine and snorted so that natives, through hallucinations, traveled to a world where they bargained with gods and devilish spirits. Even today, the Cuna Indians in Panama burn chiles at a ceremony held for girls who have reached puberty because they believe that the smoke will exorcise bad spirits.

During the Mayan period of greatness, about thirty different kinds of chile were cultivated and eaten mostly with corn, but also with turkey and cocoa drinks. The food culture of the Mayan people still exists today in the form of tortillas, the thin corn pancacke which is filled with beans and spiced with chiles. This spice followed the Mayans throughout their lives—in their food, in their religion, and in their daily habits. The native women's trick of rubbing their breasts with chiles is probably the most effective method of weaning infants (I wouldn't recommend it to mothers today, however!).

The Aztecs not only gave us the name chile, but also enriched the food culture of Mexico with dishes like ceviche, tamales, and *mole*, the well-known national sauce, which contains several different chiles.

The Aztec's first contact with the Europeans was extremely heated. When the Spaniard Herman Cortes, together with his soldiers, met the Aztec ruler Montezuma, they were greeted with cauldrons which were already boiling and spiced with chiles. The Aztecs were patiently waiting for the last ingredients—The invaders! Cortes didn't want to risk being eaten alive, and so they attacked, which led to victory—and the cauldrons being cooked dry!

Today, however, "Montezuma's revenge" has quite another meaning.

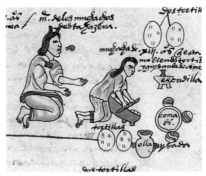

Aztec girl is taught how to grind corn and chile pepper

Christopher "Capsicum" Columbus and Others

In 1492, Christopher Columbus sailed from the port of Palos in southern Spain with hopes of finding both a new route to India and the important trade commodities—gold and pepper. He certainly found gold, but the country he believed to be India was, as most people know, the West Indies and America and the pepper was chile pepper. Columbus mistook chile for pepper, and that is the reason there is the misleading notion of "Spanish pepper" in Europe. In his log book Columbus recorded that he had found the spices he had been looking for, which was not true.

One correct observation Columbus made, however, was that the natives used spices in their cooking. Fortunately, he took chiles back to Europe with him.

Columbus was welcomed with open arms by King Ferdinand and Queen Isabella upon his return to Barcelona, where he presented them with gifts of gold, native handicrafts, and chiles in large sacks.

Unwittingly, Columbus was the catalyst for the distribution of what would become the most widely-used spice in the world.

The first chile plants to arrive in Spain came from the West Indies and were used primarily as decoration. However, the lack of a warm and humid climate meant the plants did not do very well. Thanks to the Portuguese, however, the chile was eventually distributed worldwide.

Spain and Portugal were not officially at war with each other, yet there was enormous prestige involved in the struggle for economic and territorial world domination, a sort of "cold war" in the Middle Ages. The Portuguese had begun to exploit West Africa and had been around the Cape of Good Hope in the pursuit of finding trade routes to India and the rest of Asia. This was enough to make Isabella, the Spanish queen, send of her trump card (Columbus) in a westward direction! However in 1498 the Portuguese took the lead once again, when Vasco da Gama took the first step on true Indian soil.

At the same time, Pope Alexander VI tried to end the feud between the two Iberian nations by dividing the world map from north to south through the Atlantic. Spain was given access to the west including the South American continent, and Portugal the east, including Africa, the all-important India, and the rest of Asia, with even a bit of Brazil as we know it today. Portugal strengthened its position further when Alfonso de Albuquerque, in 1510, conquered the Muslim-dominated Goa in India, and Lisbon took over as the most important trade center after Venice. In addition, Spain began to lose interest in her colonies when the gold ran out. The Portuguese saw their chance and created a trade route between South America, Europe, Africa, and Asia. This resulted in the rapid distribution of chiles between the continents.

SILIQVASTRVM MAIVS ET MINVS   Calchutischer Pfeffer.

The Portuguese now cultivated chile and corn in their African colonies, which shortened transit considerably. Chiles were rapidly accepted by Africans, who loved the spicy addition to their monotonous, starchy food. David Livingston, the British explorer who expanded Europe's knowledge of Africa, managed to survive there on meat spiced with chile, and described ow African women bathed in water in which they had added round chile to increase their powers of attraction.

Chiles were distributed in Asia by the Portuguese and Asians ia established trade convoys at sea. They were integrated very quickly into food cultures which already had access to a wealth of spices. In India and Thailand, ginger and black pepper were already being used to give curry, masala, chutney, and stir-fry cooking more flavor; now cooking was brought to perfection thanks to the chile. Another explanation for the chile's popularity is that Asiatic countries—India, for example—have traditionally based their cookery upon the strength of its flavor as part of their cultural food heritage.

The final stage of the chile's circumnavigation of the world begin in the Philippines, where the young, tender leaves of the chile plant are used in cooking. Spanish descendants in the New World established a trade route between Manila and Acapulco, Mexico. The chile returned to where it originated!

Chile Becomes Paprika

But how did the chile reach Europe?

Arabian merchants took chiles with them from Goa, which was the center of the spice trade in India, to the Middle East and North Africa, and from there it was distributed during the sixteenth century via the Ottoman Empire, to eastern Europe. In southern Hungary, slaves in the Turkish army first planted and cultivated chiles in the 1700s.

Shepherds and farmers were the first to use chiles in cooking and slowly but surely, the new spice reached the tables of the upper class. This route was quite different from the use of other spices, which were first established among the wealthy.

Myths and legends are also part of the chile. In Zoltan Halasz's, *Hungarian Paprika Through the Ages*, a beautiful Hungarian girl is forced into a Turkish harem in Buda. At night, she creeps out into the garden of the harem to rendezvous with her lover, and it is there where she also learns the secrets of chile cultivation. When the Christian troops invade the town and the Turks retreat, it is the Hungarian girl who gives the gardeners their first paprika seeds and it is these seeds which are sown on the slopes of Buda.

Denzli, in southwest Turkey, is known for its chile pepper plantation.

Goulash and paprikas (Hungarian national dishes) are made with sweet, minced, or ground paprika. The word *paprika* is from the Latin *piper*, which means pepper; in Hungary, paprika describes all kinds of chiles.

In southern and central Europe, chiles were distributed during the latter part of the sixteenth century mostly by botanists and gardeners, who cultivated everything they could get hold of from the New World. However, chiles were also used in farm cookery. Emperor Maximilian's court botanist, Clusius, noted that "Capsicum is frequently cultivated in Castile (Spain) by both gardeners and farmers. Capsicum is used both dried or fresh and green, as a spice instead of black pepper all year round. There are an incredible number of varieties. . . ."

Otherwise, the sea route was the most common form of travel for imports to Venice, Lisbon, and Antwerp, which were major ports. In Italy, however, the tomato, which is related to the chile, became more popular except in Calabria, on Italy's "pointed toe." Even today, fish, meat, and vegetables are spiced with pepperoncini, which is also used in pickling.

In the 1600s, Holland received its fair share of chiles

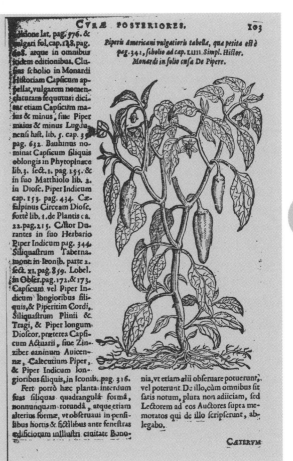

Illustration by C. Clusius, 1601

thanks to its Indonesian colonies. Although typical Dutch food is not spicy, chiles have nevertheless been a distinguishing characteristic; the cultivation of Dutch chiles and bell peppers is widely appreciated. Indonesian cuisine, which is known for *rijstaffel*, a rice buffet with *sambal* (a ground chile paste) and *satay* (grilled meat on a skewer) is also representative of Holland's cuisine.

23

The fact that Sweden's famed botanist, Carl Linnaeus, has had such an influence on chiles is perhaps not so well known, but in his pioneering work, *Species Plantarum* (1753) he gives the chile two names—a generic family name and a specific name for the species. Linnaeus upheld here for the first time that Capsicum is the genus for all chiles and also names two species, *C. annuum* and *C. frutescens*.

Chile, "the drug," was mostly used in Swedish pharmacology at this time. An attempt was made to cultivate chiles, and it was used together with one of the most important everyday items at that time. Linnaeus writes, "Capsicum grew here (in Malmo), large and luxuriant and ripe under the open sky. This Spanish pepper was bought by the local inhabitants and placed in weak vodka or schnapps so that it would have a sharper taste as if it were actually stronger, but which was actually a deception." There really was a predecessor to Absolut Chile!

Spicy Mistakes

Paprika, Spanish pepper, and red pepper are just a few of the many names for chiles. All of these names allude to the Latin name *Piper nigrum*, or black pepper, which is partly Columbus's fault. Capsicum is the correct genus for chile (which comes from the Greek word, *kapsi*, meaning to bite). To clarify these misnomers, let's go back to the time before Columbus landed on America's shores.

The chile-growing Arawak Indians called the beloved spice *axi*. It was changed in the Spanish language to *aji*, which is still used today in Spain, Latin America, and South America. Columbus, struck with wonder, believed the shiny red pepper to be a special kind of peppercorn and gave it the name *pimiento*, or pepper.

The Portuguese coined the phrase "Spanish pepper" when they took over the world trade for red pepper. In parts of Africa, chile was called *piri piri*, which means pepper in Swahili.

Cherry pepper and wax chile at the market hall in Budapest.

The Greek seafarers called chiles "peperi" which has changed to pepperoni or feferoni; in Italian, it is called *peperone* or pepperoncini.

Due to the expansion of the Ottoman Empire in the Balkans and in Hungary, the chile's name changed all the time: From *peperke*, *piperke*, and *paperke* in Bulgaria to paprika in Hungary.

In the English language, fresh paprika is called bell pepper and ground paprika is just paprika. Chiles in England are called chillis but in the U.S. they are called chili, chile, or chile pepper. Certain chiles change their names once they are dried. Does this sound complicated?

Chile originated in the language and culture of the Aztecs and today has its strongest foothold in Mexico and the American Southwest. In Fort Worth, Texas, there is even an institute devoted to the publication of *The Chile Pepper Magazine*.

But don't be too frustrated by all the names given to the chile because one thing is certain: We find many names for the one we love!

Beautiful wreaths of chiles in Santa Fe, New Mexico.

A Chile Presentation

Hot Profiles

The Scoville test determines the strength of a chile. The method, which tests flavors, was developed in 1912 by pharmacist W. L. Scoville. The capsaicin in chile is mixed with a certain amount of alcohol, which is then diluted with sugar until the strength is almost unnoticeable. The test is subjective but very accurate. However, it has recently been replaced by a more modern technique, HPLC, or High Pressure Liquid Chromatography, which gives a more exact result. The capsaicin is isolated and measured and also converted into Scoville units.

Here are some of the most common types of chiles, with their internationally accepted names:

Ancho/Poblano

Color: Maroon to dark brown-black
Shape: Flat, shriveled, and wide
Size: 5 to 6 inches in length and 2 to 3 inches wide
Strength: Mild to slightly hot; 1,000 to 1,500 Scoville units
Usage: Ancho has a characteristic taste of cocoa, coffee, and dried fruit. Ancho, together with chile pasilla and chile mulato, creates "the holy trinity," which is what the traditional Mexican mole sauces are based upon. Besides being used in moles, ancho is excellent in barbecue sauces, giving them a deep red color. Ancho compliments game, pork, poultry, and salmon, and even chocolate desserts.
General: Ancho chile means wide chile and does, in fact, refer to its shape. Chile poblano is the fresh fruit which is called ancho chile when it is dried. This popular chile represents about one-fifth of all chiles consumed in Mexico.

Anaheim

Chilaca

Poblano

Turkish Aci Sivri

Dutch

Hungarian Wax

Cubanelle

Güero

Jalapeño

Hot Wax

Habanero

Green Thai

Yellow Thai

Cherry

Red Thai

Serrano

Paloma

California

New Mexican

Ancho

South American Aji

Pasilla

Costeño

Asian Cayenne

Habanero

Morita

Chipotle

Italian Diavolitu

Cascabel

Piri Piri

Cayenne

Color: Dark green to red
Shape: Elongated and curved
Size: 5 to 6 inches long and approximately ¼ to ½ inch wide
Strength: Extremely hot; 30,000 to 50,000 Scoville units
Usage: Cayenne is normally used in Louisiana cooking and in Cajun and Creole cooking. Cayenne is appreciated more for its strength than its actual taste. Ground cayenne has a delayed hot effect so beware! Soups, sauces, casseroles, marinades, and dressings should be spiced carefully with cayenne so it won't be unbearably strong.
General: Cayenne was probably named after the town, or the river of the same name in the French Guyana, but it is neither cultivated there nor anywhere else in South America. Portuguese seafarers took cayenne back with them to Europe and later, to Africa, India, and the rest of Asia. It is grown commercially in the U.S. In Louisiana, cayenne is known for lending its own particularly strong touch to the state's "red gold" hot sauce. Cayenne has also become synonymous with dried chile in powdered form, which does not necessarily contain only cayenne.

Cayenne is used symbolically as a kind of insult. "Go to where the pepper grows," which literally means "Go to hell," refers to the town of Cayenne and its unhealthy climate.

Cherry pepper

Color: Green to red
Shape: Round like a cherry
Size: 1 to 2 inches in diameter
Strength: Sweet and mild to hot; 100 to 3,500 Scoville units
Usage: Cherry pepper is extremely popular in the U. S., Hungary, and the Balkans, where it is pickled and served on the side. Fresh cherry pepper is also suitable for use in sauces, salsas, salads, and casseroles. The cherry pepper is appreciated for its sweet, fruity, hot flavor.
General: There are many varieties of cherry pepper in all sizes and strengths (e.g., Hungary cherry, cherry jubilee, or Christmas cherry). In addition to cooking cherry peppers, you can make decorative braids and garlands with them.

Chipotle (smoked jalapeño)

Color: Pale maroon to coffee brown
Shape: Shriveled and irregularly shaped
Size: 2 to 4 inches long and approximately ½ to ¾ inch wide
Strength: Medium to hot; 2,500 to 5,000 Scoville units
Usage: Hot, smoky, earthy, sweet, tobacco, and cocoa all describe the taste of the chipotle. It is excellent with game and pork, and even with oily fish, like salmon. Chipotle is suitable for use in marinades, soups, salsas, dressings, barbecue sauces, and breads.
General: The Aztecs are supposed to have given the chipotle its name, as it is the same name they use for the process of smoking and drying chiles. Normally, fresh red jalapeño is used for smoking, but other types of jalapeño are smoked as well. Mora or morita are two such varieties with a similar taste. Chipotle is used generously in American Southwestern cookery. In Mexico, it constitutes one-fifth of jalapeños produced. Chipotle is sold dried or as a canned or bottled paste, as hot sauce, or pickled in adobo sauce, which consists of vinegar, garlic, onion, tomato purée, and spices.

Dutch Chile

Color: Green or red
Shape: Cylindrical, slightly curved and tapered
Size: 4 inches long and ¾ to 1 inch wide
Strength: Medium to hot; 2,500 to 5,000 Scoville units
Usage: The green fruit is somewhat bitter with an unripe taste and strength. The fully ripened red chile has a richer strength and slight sweetness. Dutch chile is great with seafood, poultry, and meat, or in soups, salsas, chutneys, and desserts.
General: The Dutch chile is one of the most common types of chile and is available fresh, all year round. Dutch chile is a hybrid, created in the Dutch greenhouse, but it was probably cultivated in Indonesia originally. It is similar to cayenne, but is nowhere near as hot.

Habanero

Color: Green, orange, or red
Shape: Irregular, round, and blunt; sometimes pointed
Size: 1 to 2 inches long and 1 to 2 inches wide
Strength: Super hot; 100,000 to 300,000 Scoville units. In the autumn of 1994, the Chile Institute announced that a certain variety of habanero had been calculated as measuring 577,000 Scoville units.

Usage: Habanero is an extremely popular ingredient in hot sauce, but can be paired very successfully with fish, shellfish, pork, and fowl. Habanero is wonderful in soups, salsas, chutneys, dressings, marinades, and breads.

Habanero is appreciated for its incredible strength and tropical fruity taste.

General: Habanero, meaning "from Havana," is mostly cultivated on the Mexican peninsula, the Yucatán, in Belize, and now even in Dutch greenhouses. That it is the world's hottest chile is unmistakable and one should handle it with great care. Habanero is up to 100 times hotter than jalapeño. This is the chile which separates the men from the boys!

Hungarian sweet chile

Color: Dark red
Shape: Long and wide, with rounded tip
Size: 5 to 6 inches long and 2 inches wide
Strength: Sweet and mild; 0 to 100 Scoville units
Usage: Can be filled as a chile relleno or used in salads, soups, casseroles, and as a fried vegetable. Hungarian sweet chiles are appreciated for their full-bodied sweet aroma. They are an ingredient in Ajvar (see page 78), a terrific tangy chile dip.
General: Hungarian sweet pepper is grown in Hungary and eastern Europe, but can also be found in California. With its dense flesh, it is similar to a bell pepper but with a riper, rounder taste. During harvesting in September and October you can, with a little luck, buy fresh Hungarian sweet chiles even as far north as Sweden. If you cannot get fresh chiles, look for the pickled kind.

Hungarian wax chile

Color: Pale green-yellow, or yellow to red
Shape: Cylindrical, long, curved, and tapered
Size: 5 to 6 inches long and 1 inch wide
Strength: From sweet and mild to hot; 5,000 to 10,000 Scoville units

Hungarian
wax chile

Usage: A favorite Hungarian gastronomic delight eaten pickled, served on the side, or filled with goat cheese. Nice and crisp in salads or delicious in salsas, casseroles, and soups. Wax chile is greatly appreciated for its beautiful yellow color and its full rich taste.

General: The wax chile has been named after its bright and shiny surface. It can vary in strength; the mild kind in the U.S. is known as banana pepper. This variety first came from Hungary in 1932, where other varieties such as Hungarian Yellow, Wax Hot, Gold Spike, and Santa Fe Grande were developed from the original plant. Hungarian Wax Chile is available from late summer to autumn in many produce markets and market halls.

Jalapeño

Jalapeño

Color: Light green, dark green to red
Shape: Cylindrical, with a somewhat blunt tip
Size: 2 to 2½ inches long and approximately 1 inch wide
Strength: Medium hot to hot; 2,500 to 5,000 Scoville units
Usage: As a snack pickled in vinegar, oil, and spices. Can be used in salsas, salads, sauces, chutneys, and casseroles; even used in desserts and breads. Jalapeño has the flavor of a green vegetable blessed with full-bodied strength and sweetness.

General: Jalapeño is originally from Mexico and takes its name from the town of Jalapa in the state of Veracruz. It is one of the world's most popular chiles; even in Sweden, we have learned how to pronounce the name correctly. The jalapeño has also become one of the most commercially successful chiles, and is a symbol for "hot and spicy cooking" in Texas and its environs. Try candy, ice cream, jelly or mustard flavored with jalapeño or look for decorations and ornaments with a chile theme. Souvenirs with cult status!

The astronaut Bill Lenoir had such a passion for jalapeño that it became the first chile to reach outer space, a hot capsule on board the spaceship Columbia in 1982.

New Mexican chile. These brown fruits are called chocolate in technical terminology.

New Mexican

Color: Green or red
Shape: Oblong, rather flat, with rounded tip
Size: Approximately 8 to 10 inches long and 1 to 2 inches wide
Strength: Mild, medium, or hot; 500 to 10,000 Scoville units
Usage: With its varying strength and full-bodied vegetable sweetness, the New Mexican chile is great for different types of cooking and adds a fantastic color to salsa. It is much appreciated in barbecue sauces, casseroles, and soups, or for chile rellenos (see page 90).
General: No other chile has created so many problems with its many different names; Anaheim, California, long green, and long red chile are but a few of them. The New Mexican chile was grown originally in New Mexico, but the seeds were transferred to California, where it was grown commercially at the start of this century. Because of its nearness to the town of Anaheim, this particular chile shared the same name for many years. During this time, the cultivation of the chile was developed in New Mexico and it eventually resumed its correct name, the New Mexican chile. Today, this chile is no longer grown in Anaheim, but it has become a symbol of the state of New Mexico. A great tradition in New Mexico is to hang a braid or wreath of chiles—a *ristra*—in the kitchen or on your front door to signify "welcome to my home."

Fresh green New Mexican chiles have six times the amount of vitamin C contained in an orange.

Bell Pepper (Paprika)

Color: Green, yellow, orange, red, or dark purple
Shape: Wide, round, and cone-shaped
Size: 4 to 6 inches long and 3 to 4 inches wide
Strength: Sweet and mild; 0 to 500 Scoville units
Usage: The bell pepper is one of our staple vegetables; it is appreciated raw, stuffed, or filled in different ways. The bell pepper is also suitable for most dishes where a touch of color is needed, for example, salsas, soups, and salads. However, the bell pepper comes into its own when it

is roasted and peeled with the seeds removed. Hungarian cooks use ground dried bell pepper, or paprika, in two ways: The paprika is added to flour and roasted in cooking fat to make a so-called roux, which is then used for thickening and seasoning sauces and soups. Or, the paprika is added to chopped onion which is fried in oil and then mixed with other ingredients. When it is prepared in this way, it is called goulash or paprikas (savory Hungarian dishes).

General: The bell pepper is a large chile and our most popular Capsicum. The green pepper has a more stringent and somewhat bitter taste compared to the riper, sweet, yellow and red peppers. In Europe, fresh bell peppers are produced mostly in Holland, Spain, and Hungary, while the paprika we use comes mostly from the U.S. and Hungary. Paprika is produced from ripe red bell peppers which have been finely chopped and are then dried in an oven. After that, they are ground into powder.

In Hungary, there was a national scandal concerning paprika in 1994. Newspapers disclosed that some paprika had been colored with a red substance, iron-oxide, which is used to protect ships made of steel from rusting. The color had been used to make cheap Romanian and Ukrainian paprika look more authentic (these powders do not have the same intense red color as the Hungarian kind). Iron oxide is poisonous.

Twenty people were hospitalized and the police confiscated hundreds of kilos of paprika. Two paprika warehouses were raided by the police and seventeen people were arrested on suspicion of tampering with or faking paprika. In Hungary, where 6,000 tons of paprika are manufactured every year and Jancsi Paprika is the national symbol, one cannot produce fake paprika without risking dire punishment!

Pasilla

Color: Dark brown to black
Shape: Long, flat, tapered, wrinkly, and with pronounced tip
Size: 6 to 11 inches long and ½ to 1 inch wide
Strength: Medium hot; 1,000 to 15,000 Scoville units
Usage: Pasilla is always used in mole, but it also excellent in other sauces, especially for shellfish, because of its fine rich, red color and aromatic strains of raisins, berries, herbs, cocoa, and licorice.
General: Pasilla is the dried chile; it is called Chilaca chile when fresh. The dried chile has been given the name Pasilla due to its raisinlike color. The chile is used mostly dried or pulverized.

35

Pepperoncini/Pepperoni

Color: Green to red and yellowish-green
Shape: Cylindrical, elongated, wrinkly, with noticeable spots
Size: 2 to 3 inches long and ¼ to ½ inch wide
Strength: Mild to medium hot; 100 to 1,500 Scoville units
Usage: Good in salads, salsas, casseroles, with fish and seafood, and pickled. Dried, it is used coarsely ground as pizza pepper. With its varying strength and sweetness, this chile is a favorite ingredient in Calabian and Sicilian cookery of southern Italy.
General: The name comes from the Italian word for chile, *peperone*. The Greek variety, Golden Greek, is well-known as pepperoni, pickled in vinegar, and as a common accompaniment to kebab. The yellow-green variety is the highest quality chile of all the different kinds of pepperoni.

Piri piri

Color: Green or red
Shape: Small, cylindrical, and tapered
Size: ½ to 1 inch long and ⅛ inch wide
Strength: Extremely hot; 125,000 to 150,000 Scoville units
Usage: Piri piri is used in Portugal in domestic hot sauces and pickled in vinegar. It is great in casseroles, and with chicken or fish. Piri piri is appreciated for its hot taste.
General: The Portuguese introduced this little hot chile to its African colonies, where it was given its name. Piri piri is also the name of Mozambique's national dish, which consists of prawns, fish, or chicken accompanied by a piri piri sauce.

Serrano

Color: Green or red, shiny
Shape: Cylindrical, tapered with a blunt tip
Size: 1 to 2 inches long and ¼ to ½ inch across
Strength: Hot to extremely hot; 10,000 to 23,000 Scoville units
Usage: With its crisp, fresh, hot taste, Serrano chiles are great in salsas, guacamole, ceviche, and as Mexican pickles.
General: In Spanish, serrano means "from the mountains;" the chile has its origins north of Puebla and Hidalgo in Mexico. Today it grows in numerous places and altitudes. Serrano is, together with jalapeño, one of the most popular chiles in Mexico and America's Southwest. The yearly production in Mexico averages 180,000 tons.

Tabasco

Color: Green-yellow to yellow, orange, and red
Shape: Tiny, elongated, cylindrical, with pointed tip
Size: ½ to 1 inch long and ⅛ to ½ inch across
Strength: Extremely hot; 30,000 to 50,000 Scoville units
Usage: The Tabasco chile is used, above all, in hot sauce, but can also be used in salsas, soups, casseroles, and wok cookery. The Tabasco is appreciated for its pungent strong flavor; it can be substituted with the Thai chile.
General: The name comes from the Mexican federal state, Tabasco, where trade took place with New Orleans during the mid-1800s. Avery Island, Louisiana, is the birthplace of this chile. Here, Edmund McIlhenny sowed the first seeds of something that was to become the world's most famous hot sauce: Tabasco brand pepper sauce.

Thai

Color: Light green to red
Shape: Elongated and pointed
Size: 1 inch long and ⅛ inch across
Strength: Extremely hot; 50,000 to 100,000 Scoville units
Usage: The Thai chile has become synonymous with Thai cooking; it gives a bite to curry paste, wok cookery, and domestic hot sauces. Thai chile is mostly appreciated for its heat—so be careful!
General: The Thai chile first came to Thailand and the rest of Southeast Asia after Columbus discovered it in America. There are many unnamed varieties of Thai chile in Southeast Asia, which instead are characterized by their size, pungency, color, freshness, dryness, or powdered form.

Tomato chile

Color: Green to red
Shape: Round, like a tomato
Size: 2 inches in diameter
Strength: Sweet and mild; 0 to 500 Scoville units.
Usage: Can be used like a bell pepper in all types of cooking. Dried Tomato chile is ground and sold as Spanish paprika powder. In Hungary and in the Balkans, it is stuffed with sauerkraut and pickled.

General: The Tomato chile probably originated in Central America. It is cultivated today in Morocco, Spain, and Hungary, where it is also used as a natural food additive, oleoresin.

Tomato chiles growing on plantations in the Murcia region of southeast Spain. They are dried, pulverized, and sold as Spanish paprika.

Starting to get hungry now? Before you begin, read the following instructions describing equipment, technique, and ingredients. To create a successful dish, it's important to be equipped with good kitchen tools and perfect ingredients. Sharp knives, a large cutting board, a pepper grinder, teflon pans to minimize the use of fat, and a food processor are all good investments.

In the same way, fresh herbs growing in the kitchen window, sea salt or kosher salt, a few assorted oils and vinegars, and a selection of rice, grains, and beans as well as sambal and hot sauces are indispensable assets in the kitchen. A good homemade broth or stock is an unbeatable ingredient for achieving tasty, appetizing dishes.

Do be particular about quality. Fresh chicken is better than frozen, fresh mushrooms are more fun to use than the canned kind. If you can't find the right type of chile for the recipes, they can, in most cases, be replaced by a hot sauce, sambal, or other chile product. Last, but not least, read the recipes thoroughly and make large batches to freeze. And remember, a good cook must always be hungry!

When you buy chiles, they should smell fresh and invigorating. The red chiles are normally stronger and more pungent than the green ones and you can always reduce the strength in the recipes by removing the seeds and ribs. If you do not plan to use the chiles immediately, you can store them in a well-sealed plastic bag or plastic container with a lid, and they will keep for four weeks or more in the refrigerator.

Dried chiles can be bought in small bundles, chile wreaths, or in a bag. Dried chiles should be clean, with a deep, clear color, and free from insect invasion. Ground chile, or paprika, should have a clean aroma and a fine, deep color.

Dried chiles can be roasted on low heat in an oven or in a frying pan to bring out the flavor and aroma. The chiles can then be soaked in water, after removing the stalks, seeds, ribs, and skin. Purée the chiles in a food processor to a paste—the paste will give a great color and a hot, appetizing flavor to salsas, barbecue sauces, and casseroles.

In several of the recipes, **fresh roasted chiles** are used, which is an interesting way of enhancing the flavor in different dishes. Bell peppers and other chiles with thick skins are most suitable for roasting. The easiest way is to put them in the oven with the temperature set to 450 degrees. Position the chiles directly on the rack for 30 to 45 minutes, turning them over a few times until the skin is almost black. Put the roasted fruits in a plastic bag which can be sealed, or in a plastic jar with a lid, so that they can steam in their own heat for about 30 minutes. When they have cooled off, the skin is easily peeled off with a knife. Divide the chiles and remove the seeds, the ribs, and stalks.

If you have a gas stove you can roast chiles over the flames until the skins are black. In the summertime, simply put them on the barbecue grill to blacken.

If you want to stuff chiles, do it this way: Make a cut in the side and take out the seeds and ribs but leave the stems.

Please note: When handling chiles, I recommend that you use plastic gloves, or rinse your hands often in water, to protect yourself from the capsaicin. Don't rub your eyes, or touch any other sensitive parts of the body after preparing chiles.

I love roasted **garlic** with its rounder, milder taste. Roast a whole head of garlic, leaving the skin on the cloves, at 350 degrees for 40 to 50 minutes. When the garlic is soft and sweet, it is done.

Shallots are roasted for the same reason as garlic. Keep the skin on and roast at 350 degrees for 35 to 40 minutes.

Tomatoes are also suitable for roasting. The flavor is concentrated once the juice evaporates. Cut the tomatoes across and place them on a rack in a 300 degree oven for at least 90 minutes.

If you have a kitchen scale available, it is good to use for weighing the dry ingredients in baking and dessert recipes. Food which is measured in ounces is always more exact.

Red ripe jalapeños are highly appreciated, mostly by Mexico. The chile peppers are dried and smoked and renamed chipotle chiles.

Ingredients

Apple cider vinegar is made from apple cider and has a rich flavor and aroma of apple. Suitable in dressings, marinades, sauces, glazes, and cooked salsas.

Arrowroot is ground from tropical American arrowroot plants with starchy tuberous roots. A clear thickening agent.

Balsamic vinegar is made from Italian red wine, and is smooth and mild but with a great deal of flavor. Aged in oak barrels for 2 to 40 years. Can be used with great success in salsas, dressings, and hot sauces.

Black beans are black on the outside and dark purple on the inside. Grown and used in Latin America, South America, and in the Caribbean. Black beans have a wonderful flavor and taste great with chiles.

Cannellini beans are a variety of white bean or kidney bean. Greatly appreciated in Italy. As with all beans, they are best cooked on low heat and covered. Available in health food stores and market halls.

Canola oil is extracted from the canola seed and has a neutral taste and high level of linoleic acid, a polyunsaturated fatty acid. Canola can be used in cooking and in cold dishes.

Chile pepper ground, ancho style, is a pure chile product consisting of several types of chile grown in the valleys of Santa Maria in California.

Chile powder is a mixture of mild chile, cumin, oregano, and garlic. The blend was concocted by Texas immigrants as a seasoning for chili con carne.

Cilantro belongs to the parsley family and is the most commonly used herb in the world. Cilantro, or fresh coriander, has an intense, soapy taste which provides a nice contrast to chile. Use the chopped leaves for flavoring salsas, marinades, salads, meats, poultry, fish, and shellfish. Cilantro cannot be replaced with dried coriander.

Corn flour has a yellow color and characteristic flavor, not to be confused with maizena (cornstarch). There is also blue, white, red, and purple corn flour made from Indian corn. Corn flour is either finely or coarsely ground. Finely ground corn flour is used for bread and coatings; the coarsely ground kind is used for tortillas.

Corn oil is extracted by pressing corn sprouts, which contain forty to fifty percent fat. The sprouts have a high level of unsaturated fatty acid. Corn oil can be used in cooking and in cold dishes.

Couscous is a grain made from durum wheat. It is also the name of the national dish in Tunisia. Available in health food stores, market halls, and specialty grocery stores.

Cumin is not to be confused with caraway seeds. Ground cumin has a strong aroma and a faint, earthy, sour flavor. Use sparingly in cooking so it doesn't overwhelm the dish. Whole cumin, however, does have a somewhat milder taste. Cumin also plays an important part in spicy curry blends and garam masala, and is often combined with ground chile pepper.

Ginger has its origin in Asia where it has been cultivated for over 3,000 years. Today it also grows in the West Indies, Africa, Australia, and Hawaii. Ginger is available fresh, dried, ground, preserved, and candied. It has a strong, acidic, aromatic flavor with a flowery sweetness. Ginger should be firm and juicy. The young, delicate stem of the ginger plant is considered to be the best quality (it is less thready). Gingerin is the strong substance in ginger which, in the same way that capsaicin influences chiles, gives a kick to cooking.

Green chile flakes are dried flakes of Anaheim chile, a variety of the New Mexican chile. The flakes have a mild aroma and can be used for almost everything. Available at wholesalers.

The **green onion** is a small, thin, onion, resembling a miniature leek, with a nice, mild onion taste. It is suitable for salads, in salsas, and as a garnish for chili and other spicy dishes.

Hot sauce, or chile sauce as it is also called, is based on the chile. Louisiana is known for its hot sauce products, based on Cayenne and Tabasco chiles. All chile-loving countries worldwide produce their own domestic hot sauces, often based on local chiles. A chile sauce with a pure chile flavor is a good second choice, if you cannot find fresh chiles.

Ibarra chocolate is a dark Mexican chocolate flavored with cinnamon and almonds. Together with chiles they make up the classic national sauce: mole. Available in Mexican specialty stores.

Kritharaki is a Greek pasta made of durum wheat; it is called *orzo* in Italian. Looks like large grains of rice.

Lemongrass is a tropical grass with a clean aroma and lemon taste. It is used in Asia more than anywhere else. The lower part is used whole or as a paste for seasoning pork, chicken, fish, and shellfish. Available in Asian specialty stores.

Lima beans originated in tropical America. The somewhat smaller beans are usually sweeter in taste.

Lime is a small green relative of the lemon. The best quality are the Mexican or the Florida Key limes, which have a dark green color with touches of yellow. These limes should not be confused with the kaffir lime, which is only used for its skin and leaves.

Liquid smoke is a liquid concentration of smoky, woody flavors (e.g., mesquite and hickory). Available in a bottle, it is used for seasoning stocks, broths, and marinades.

Mascarpone is a creamy Italian cheese made from thick, sour cream. Mascarpone is used to make the popular Italian dessert, tiramisu.

Mozzarella is a fresh, mild cheese from southern Italy. The most famous is the *mozzarella di bufalo* which is made of buffalo milk. If mozzarella is made from cow's milk, it is called *fior di latte*.

Okra is a vegetable-hibiscus with a neutral, rugged flavor. It secretes a milky gel when cooked and is, therefore, excellent for thickening sauces.

Peanut oil has a wonderful flavor and is high in linoleic acid, a polyunsaturated fatty acid. It is able to withstand high frying temperatures and is used especially in the Asian kitchen (e.g., stir-fry cooking). Approximately fifteen percent of the world's production of vegetable oils are derived from the peanut. Available in Asian stores.

Pecans are produced in Texas, New Mexico, and Georgia, as well as Mexico. The pecan is a relative to the walnut and is very popular in southern cooking. Pecan wood is used as charcoal for barbecues.

Phyllo pastry is a thin, leafy dough made of flour and water. Ideal for pastries such as strudel and baklava, but also in meatier pirogies, samosas, and pies. Phyllo dough is available frozen in specialty grocery stores, market halls, and Greek delis.

Pinto beans are a variety of white bean. Pinto means "painted" in Spanish. The bean is beige with pink streaks, and when it is cooked it turns a brownish pink. Pinto beans have a neutral flavor and are easily combined with other ingredients.

Raw sugar is most often made from sugar cane and is less refined than white sugar. Available in health food stores.

Red kidney beans are primarily used in North American and are popular in Tex-Mex cooking. They are an important ingredient in chili.

Rice vinegar has a mild flavor with low acidity and natural sweetness. Very tasty in salsas and dressings.

Sambal is a liquid chile paste. It originated in Indonesia where it is served as a table seasoning. Sambal is based on the Indonesian chile, lombok, which is similar to the Tabasco, Cayenne, or the great Thai chile. You can make your own sambal using Dutch chiles mixed with fruit, nuts, fresh herbs, garlic, or other spices. Examples of commercial sambals are oelek, badjak, manis, trassi, asem, and kemiri.

Sea salt has a very mild, pleasant taste. Available in coarser grains suitable for salt grinders and also as finer crystals that can be crumbled with the fingers. Sea salt is suitable in salads, salsas, and gives a perfect final touch to meat, fish, and vegetables. Has a lower sodium content than regular salt.

Star anise is the fruit of the magnolia tree. It is picked and sun-dried before it ripens. It isn't related to fennel or anise, but it does have a similar, if stronger, more aromatic taste. The beautiful eight-pointed star anise lends an exciting flavor to pork, chicken, fish, shellfish, and desserts, as well as complementing chiles wonderfully. Available in Asian markets.

Sun-dried tomatoes originated as prime plum tomatoes from southern Italy. They are picked at their peak of ripeness on the vine, dried, and sprinkled with a little salt. Sun-dried tomatoes have a concentrated, rich taste perfect for dressings, soups, sauces, and casseroles. Sold, reconstituted, in glass jars or dried in bags.

Tamarind looks like a wide, thick bean pod and holds a sticky fruit pulp with large seeds. Available as a canned paste with a light, sweet and sour taste. Tamarind is used as a seasoning in soups, sauces, marinades, and desserts. Available in Asian markets.

Tomatillo looks like a small green tomato with a thin, protective husk. However, the tomatillo is not related to the tomato but to the gooseberry family. It also has a similar tart, fresh, sourish taste that resembles rhubarb or unripe plums. Tomatillo is mostly used in Mexico and the American Southwest. It is excellent in salsas and sauces. Available fresh or canned.

Valrhona chocolate is often called the Rolls Royce of chocolates. Valrhona contains a high level of cacao, and has aromas of berries, fruit, flowers, tobacco, and nuts. It is made from specially selected South American and Caribbean cacao beans. The Grand Crus of chocolate is available in stores specializing in chocolate, coffee, and tea.

Virgin olive oil is cold-pressed with a rich taste and is loaded with nutrients. In Italy, the oils are divided into quality classifications: "Extra Vergine" (extra fine virgin oil) is, according to law, only allowed to have one percent of free fatty acids. "Vergine" (virgin oil) is a more ordinary type of oil with more than one percent of free fatty acids. The classification "Olio Di Oliva" (olive oil) is a warm-pressed oil that has been refined. Virgin oil is my favorite for salsas and dressings.

Hot underwear

Where to Find the Heat

Chiles are easier to find than you think! They are available fresh, dried, ground, pickled in vinegar, and in hot sauce, sambal, and salsas. Most supermarkets have an assortment of green chiles (varieties of the New Mexican chile) and jalapeños pickled in vinegar, or as hot sauce. Piri piri is pickled in vinegar or dried.

A well-stocked grocery store ought to have Cherry peppers, Tomato chiles, Pepperoni, or Tabasco chiles, all of which are available pickled in vinegar, together with a good selection of hot sauces.

Keep a lookout for fresh chiles in produce markets and market halls between July and November; this is when chiles are available in different colors, shapes, and pungency. Chile plants can even be bought during this period in flower shops and market garden centers. If you have access to ethnic markets, you will find, guaranteed, either ground, dried, or fresh chiles and all manner of chile pastes, sambals, or hot sauces.

Wholesalers and specialty-food stores sell ground chile pepper ancho style, chipotle paste, habanero sauce, red hot chile pepper flakes, ground jalapeño, green chile flakes, Anaheim, dried ancho, and New Mexican chiles.

Also, look for stores and wholesalers that sell chile products by mail-order. The following list is a good place to start *your* own chile quest:

Chiles at a market in Mexico City

Chile By Mail

Coyote Cafe General Store
132 West Water Street
Santa Fe, NM 87501
(800) 866-HOWL or
505-982-2454
Beans, chiles (including canned chiles en adobo),
Ibarra chocolate, spices, herbs, tamarind, and vinegars.

Dean and Deluca
560 Broadway
New York, NY 10012
(212) 431-1691
Chiles, oils, vinegars, beans.

Monterrey Foods
3939 Cesar Chavez Blvd.
Los Angeles, CA 90063
(213) 263-2143
Southwestern and Mexican food products.

Italco Food Products
1340 S. Cherokee Street
Denver, CO 80223
(303) 722-1882
Oils, spices, and vinegars.

Midwest Imports
1121 South Clinton
Chicago, IL 60607
(312) 939-8400
Fresh and dried chiles

In Europe:

Cool Chile Co.
Dodie Miller Unit 7
34 Bassett Road
London, W10 6JL
England

47

Mango Salsa

New Mexican Green Pipián Salsa

New Mexican Red Chile Salsa

Fresh Salsa

Lychee-Pomegranate Salsa

Red Onion-Cilantro Salsa

Salsas, Chutneys, Barbecue Sauces, Glazes & Much More

Salsa is a sauce, a dance, and a music! As a sauce, salsa has a fast tempo—if the combined sounds of jazz, rock, and rhythm and blues intrigue you, you'll love the winning combination of tomato, onion and—of course—chiles!

Trying to define salsa is not exactly easy. Salsa is unrestrained, tasty, hot. Salsa is typically served cold, freshly made, and based upon tomato, onion, and chile, just like a finely shredded or diced salad. However, salsa can also be served warm or at room temperature, and contains fruit, berries, nuts and beans, lentils, and vegetables. By roasting, grilling, and smoking the ingredients, salsa can vary in an infinite number of ways.

Furthermore, salsa is a symbol for modern, progressive cooking, with its contrasts in color, shape, flavor, and consistency. Plus, it's good for you! So let the salsa experience explode and dance on your tongue and give a wonderful rhythm to your meal!

TOMATILLO-AVOCADO SALSA
Serves 4
—

Wonderful with grilled or fried fish or seafood, and as a dip for warm corn chips.

4 to 5 fresh tomatillos, well rinsed or 3½ oz. (1 dl) salsa verde, canned

1 avocado

1 yellow onion, chopped

1 clove garlic, roasted and peeled

Juice of 1 lime

1 fresh serrano, or jalapeño chile, or 1 tablespoon pickled jalapeño chiles

Salt

Remove stems and seeds of tomatillos. Blend all the ingredients in a food processor until fairly thick. Add salt to taste and keep in a cold place.

MANGO SALSA
Serves 4
—

Choose a chile according to its taste and pungency. Jalapeño and serrano chiles have sharp flavors, which are particularly suitable with shellfish or fish.

The chipotle's smoky taste is terrific with salmon, pork, and game. Serve with warm tortilla chips.

1 mango, diced

1 green onion, thinly sliced

1 teaspoon fresh jalapeño or serrano chiles, finely chopped, chipotle paste, or chipotle en adobo

Juice of ½ lime

1 small fresh bunch cilantro, finely chopped

Salt

Mix the ingredients together in a bowl and add salt taste. Allow mixture to stand for approximately 20 minutes before serving.

RED ONION CILANTRO SALSA
Serves 6
—

Excellent with shellfish and fish, or with grilled meat.

2 red onions, thinly sliced

4 to 5 tablespoons freshly squeezed lime or lemon juice

1 small bunch of fresh cilantro, finely chopped

1 teaspoon fresh jala-
peño, serrano, or red
Dutch chile, finely
chopped

5 to 6 tablespoons extra
virgin olive oil

Salt

Mix all the ingredients together in
a bowl and taste. Let stand for 10
minutes before serving.

PEACH-CHIPOTLE SALSA
Serves 4
—

Fruity and hot!

3 peaches, thinly sliced

1 red onion, thinly sliced

Juice of 1 lime

2 teaspoons chipotle en
adobe, chopped or
chipotle paste

Salt

Mix together all the ingredients in
a bowl and taste. Refrigerate before serving.

PEAR-CASHEW NUT SALSA
Serves 4 to 6
—

Yet another salsa without tomato! I generally serve this
salsa with warm tortilla chips,
chile rellenos, or with some
favorite cheeses. Its hot, appetizing flavor is fantastic especially with game.

2 ripe, juicy pears,
diced

5 green onions, sliced

Juice of ½ lemon

1 red bell pepper,
roasted, peeled, seeded,
and diced

1 fresh Hungarian wax
chile, finely chopped

2 stalks celery, diced

1¾ ounces cashew nuts,
chopped

Salt

Mix together all the ingredients
and let sit in a cool place for 10 to
15 minutes before serving.

LYCHEE-POMEGRANATE SALSA
Serves 6
—

Hot, fresh, sweet, and sour at the same time. Full of vitamins and fiber together with contrasts in color and consistency. Pairs well with oily fish, crispy-fried duck, and chicken.

12 to 15 lychee fruits, halved, stoned, peeled, and chopped

1 pomegranate, juice and seeds

3 green onions, thinly sliced

1 fresh serrano chile, seeded and finely chopped

Juice of 1 lime

Salt

In a bowl with the lychees, cut the pomegranate in two and squeeze out the juice and seeds. Mix with the rest of the ingredients and add salt to taste.

APPLE-LINGONBERRY (OR CRANBERRY) SALSA
Serves 4 to 6
—

Lingonberries are worth paying more attention to but if they're not available, cranberries do very nicely in this unusual salsa.

1 ¼ cups (3 dl) fresh or frozen lingonberries (or cranberries)

¼ cup (¾ dl) sugar

1 yellow onion, finely chopped

2 cloves garlic, roasted, peeled, and crushed

1 apple, peeled and diced

2 tablespoons fresh jalapeño chile, finely chopped

In a bowl, combine the lingonberries or cranberries with the sugar until the sugar has dissolved. Then stir in the rest of the ingredients. Chill in a well-sealed container with a lid.

SALSA FRESCA

Rustic tomato salsa

Serves 4
—

Make this appetizing salsa from perfectly sun-ripened tomatoes, ideally Italian plum tomatoes, and serve with seafood, chicken, or tortilla chips.

2 green onions, thinly sliced

1 clove garlic, roasted, peeled, and crushed

2 large tomatoes, cut into small pieces

1 tablespoon chopped jalapeño or serrano chile

1 teaspoon salt

1 tablespoon freshly squeezed lime or lemon juice

1 tablespoon olive oil

1 small bunch fresh cilantro, finely chopped

Mix the ingredients together in a bowl and taste. Let chill before serving.

WATERMELON-RED ONION SALSA
Serves 4 to 6
—

This salsa gives grilled fish and meat an appetizing flavor.

1 1/4 cups (300 g) watermelon without seeds

1 small red onion, finely chopped

Juice of 1 lime

1 to 2 tablespoons red Dutch chile, seeded and chopped

Salt

Dice the watermelon into small, pretty cubes. Mix with the remaining ingredients and season with salt to taste. Serve immediately.

LOBSTER-ORANGE SALSA
Serves 6
—

A sumptuous salsa for your favorite fish.

2 boiled lobsters, 12 ounces each (350 g) peeled and cut into small pieces

2 oranges, in segments, with pith removed

2 cloves garlic, roasted, peeled, and crushed

3 green onions, sliced

1 fresh jalapeño chile or 2 tablespoons pickled jalapeño chile, finely chopped

Juice of 1 lime

10 leaves fresh basil, shredded

1 tablespoon olive oil

Salt

In a bowl, mix all the ingredients together and add salt to taste. Let chill for at least 15 minutes to develop the flavor.

MUSCAT GRAPE SALSA
Serves 4

—

Can be served either with fish or as a compliment to spicy sausages.

1 ½ cups (250 g) Muscat grapes, seeded

Olive oil

4 to 5 green onions, sliced

1 to 2 teaspoons red Dutch chile, finely chopped

Salt

In a pan, brown the grapes on high heat for about 30 seconds in a little oil together with the onions. Season with chile and salt. Serve warm.

ROASTED RED PEPPER SALSA
—

Pour this salsa into a bottle and put your own label on it. The salsa should be refrigerated and will keep for approximately two weeks.

1 red bell pepper, roasted, peeled, and seeded

2 cloves garlic, roasted and peeled

2 green onions, roasted and peeled

1 teaspoon sambal oelek or hot sauce

2 teaspoons freshly squeezed lemon juice

Salt

Mix all the ingredients in a food processor until the salsa is smooth. You can determine the strength yourself by increasing or reducing the amount of sambal oelek or hot sauce.

BLACK BEAN-CORN-CILANTRO SALSA
Serves 4 to 6

—

A dark-colored salsa with a mild, sweet flavor. Exquisite color contrasts go well with smoked or grilled fish and also with chicken, beef, and pork.

½ pound (2 dl) black
beans, soaked overnight

1 yellow onion, finely
chopped

1 clove garlic, finely
chopped

1 bay leaf

1 red bell pepper,
roasted, peeled, and
seeded

1 to 2 tablespoons finely
chopped pickled jala-
peño chile

1¼ cups (3 dl) fresh
corn kernels

1 to 2 green onions,
sliced

1 small bunch fresh
cilantro, finely chopped

Salt

Strain the beans and put them in
a saucepan together with the onion, garlic, and bay leaf. Cover
with cold water and season with
salt and chile. Let simmer on low
heat, covered, for 40 to 45 minutes or until soft.

Dice the bell peppers and mix
them together with the remaining
ingredients first and then with the
beans. If desired, the salsa can be
diluted with chicken broth to a
thinner consistency.

CORN-GREEN ONION-
TOMATO SALSA
Serves 4 to 6
—

A salsa without chiles? The
sweet taste of corn and the
acid from the lime is a great
contrast to hot dishes. It can
be served with almost anything.

1½ cups (3½ dl) fresh
corn kernels

Corn oil

5 green onions, thinly
sliced

2 to 3 tomatoes, diced

Juice of 1 lime

Salt

In a pan, sauté the corn kernels
in a little oil over medium heat.
Add the onions. Lower the heat
and cook gently for a minute or
two, stirring occasionally. Add
the diced tomato and season with
salt and lime. Serve warm.

WESTERN
CHIEF

NEW MEXICAN RED CHILE SALSA
Serves 6
—

Serve this salsa with warm tortilla chips, enchiladas, egg dishes, or as a pizza topping instead of tomato sauce.

10 red New Mexican chiles, dried

2 yellow onions, finely chopped

2 cloves garlic, finely chopped

Corn or canola oil

1 bay leaf

½ teaspoon ground cinnamon

Salt

1⅔ cups to 2 cups (4 to 5 dl) water

Start by carefully roasting the dried chiles in a dry frying pan over low heat, or for 5 minutes in the oven at 300 degrees. Soak them in water and remove the stalks and seeds when the peppers have softened. In a pan, fry the onions and garlic in some oil until soft. Add the chiles and the other ingredients and simmer, covered, for 20 minutes. Mix the salsa in a food processor until smooth and, if needed, add some more salt.

NEW MEXICAN GREEN PIPIÁN SALSA
Serves 6
—

The Mayan Indians created *pipián*, a sauce which gets its taste and creamy consistency from nuts and seeds. Serve this salsa hot or cold with grilled fish, shellfish, lamb, pork, or chicken.

2 yellow onions, chopped

2 cloves garlic, chopped

1⅔ cups (4 dl) chicken stock

⅔ cup (2 dl) Anaheim chile flakes or other green chile

4 to 5 fresh tomatillos or ⅓ heaping cup (1 dl) canned salsa verde

⅓ heaping cup (1 dl) green pumpkin seeds (other nuts or seeds may be substituted)

1 bunch fresh cilantro or parsley

Salt

Olive oil

In a pan, fry the onions and garlic in some oil. Add the stock and chile flakes. Simmer, covered, for 10 minutes. Pour mixture into a food processor with the tomatillos, pumpkin seeds, and cilantro. Blend to a smooth salsa and add salt if necessary.

ROASTED HOT PEPPER RAJAS SALSA
Serves 4 to 6
—

This salsa compote made with roasted bell peppers is incredibly delicious as a vegetarian dish with fresh pasta and grated parmesan cheese. It can also be served as a side dish with fish, meat, or chicken.

1 yellow onion, sliced

1 clove garlic, finely chopped

Olive oil

2 red bell peppers, roasted, peeled, and seeded

2 yellow bell peppers, roasted, peeled and seeded

3½ ounces (1 dl) tomato juice

1 teaspoon pickled jalapeño, chopped, chipotle paste, or chipotle en adobo

1 bay leaf

Salt

In a pan, sauté the onion and garlic with a little oil until soft, without browning.

Cut the bell peppers into 1 inch strips and add to the onion with the remaining ingredients. Cover and let the salsa simmer on extremely low heat for 15 minutes.

ROASTED ROMESCO SALSA
Serves 4
—

This is my own variation of a traditional Spanish sauce which is served with shellfish and fish.

3 tomatoes, roasted

3 cloves garlic, roasted and peeled

1 red bell pepper, roasted, peeled, and seeded

2 tablespoons pickled jalapeño, chopped

3½ ounces (1 dl) almonds, blanched and roasted

3 tablespoons (½ dl) balsamic vinegar

3 tablespoons (½ dl) olive oil

1 bunch parsley

Salt

Blend all the ingredients in a food processor until smooth. Can be served warm or cold.

Apple and Potato Chutney

Chutney originated in India and is traditionally made with vegetables, fresh or dried fruit, vinegar, sugar, and spices. Chutney can be served with *papadams* (Indian crispy unleavened bread), as a spicy accompaniment to fish, shellfish, poultry, meat, and vegetable dishes, or as a topping on pizza and bread. I like to use chicken broth in chutney—it gives a more rounded taste, and balances the exotic pungency of chutney.

Take advantage of what each season has to offer and make a generous amount of chutney (which can be stored in the refrigerator). It's also fun to give homemade chutney as a gift.

APPLE AND POTATO CHUTNEY
Serves 4 to 6
—

A filling accompaniment, the potato is *in* this chutney, not just on the side. Serve with grilled or fried fish, liver, chicken, and pork.

4 apples, cored and cut into wedges

16 small potatoes, boiled and cut in half

1 baby leek, sliced diagonally

⅓ cup (1 dl) raisins

⅓ cup (1 dl) sugar

Juice of 1 lemon

1 tablespoon red Dutch chile, thinly sliced

⅓ cup (1 dl) chicken stock

1 to 2 teaspoons arrowroot or cornstarch

3 tablespoons water

Bring all the ingredients to a slow boil in a large saucepan over medium heat. Simmer for a few minutes and add the arrowroot or cornstarch and water to thicken. Serve the chutney lukewarm.

59

ONION-MINT CHUTNEY
Serves 4 to 6
—

This chutney, which is wonderful with lamb, is also excellent with grilled fish and chicken.

2 yellow onions, sliced

2 cloves garlic, coarsely chopped

3 tablespoons raisins

⅓ cup sugar (1 dl)

4 tablespoons (½ dl) apple cider vinegar

¾ cup (2 dl) chicken stock

1 fresh habanero chile, seeded and thinly sliced, or 1 to 2 tablespoons habanero hot sauce

¾ to 1¼ cup (3 dl) fresh mint leaves, shredded

Salt

3 to 4 teaspoons arrowroot or cornstarch

Put all the ingredients except the starch and mint in a pan over medium heat. Cover and simmer on low heat until the onion feels soft, for about 8 minutes. Taste to see if more salt is needed and add starch dissolved in 4 tablespoons cold water to thicken. Set the pan aside and add the mint. Serve the chutney lukewarm or at room temperature.

ORANGE-CARROT CHUTNEY
Serves 4 to 6
—

A tried-and-true combination, this chutney can be served with grilled, fried, or deep-fried fish as well as chicken, pork, and game.

3 carrots, sliced diagonally in 1/4-inch (1 cm) thick pieces

1 yellow onion, quartered

1 clove garlic, finely chopped

1 fresh habanero chile, seeded and sliced or 1 to 2 tablespoons habanero hot sauce

4 dried apricots, diced coarsely

1 stick cinnamon

1/2 cup (1 dl) sugar

3 tablespoons (1/2 dl) apple cider vinegar

1 cup (2 dl) chicken stock

2 oranges, with zest, and the fruit coarsely chopped

Salt

3 to 4 teaspoons arrowroot or cornstarch

Put all the ingredients, except the oranges, in a pan over medium heat and simmer, covered, until the carrots feel soft. Add the orange. Add salt to taste. Let simmer for another minute or two and thicken well with starch dissolved in 4½ tablespoons cold water. Serve the chutney lukewarm or at room temperature.

ROASTED GARLIC AND MANGO CHUTNEY
Serves 4 to 6
—

Garlic acquires a softer, milder taste when it is roasted. This is a chutney which can be used with most dishes.

1 mango, coarsely chopped

1 to 2 tablespoons Dutch chile or great Thai chile, thinly sliced

3 tablespoons (1/2 dl) rice vinegar

1/2 cup (1 dl) sugar

1 cup (2 dl) chicken stock

3 heads garlic, approximately 50 cloves, roasted and peeled

Salt

3 to 4 teaspoons arrow-root or cornstarch

Put all the ingredients, except the garlic cloves, in a saucepan over medium heat and simmer, covered, for 5 to 10 minutes. Add the garlic. Season with salt. Add starch, dissolved in 4½ table-spoons (¾ dl) cold water, and thicken to a smooth consistency. Serve the chutney lukewarm or at room temperature.

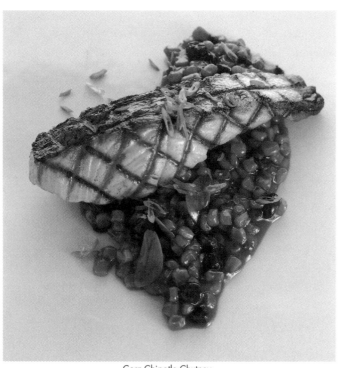

Corn-Chipotle Chutney

CORN-CHIPOTLE CHUTNEY
Serves 4 to 6

The smoky, hot taste of chipotle and the sweetness of corn and raisins makes this a real Southwestern chutney.

1¾ cups (4½ dl) fresh corn kernels

½ cup (1 dl) brown sugar

3 tablespoons (½ dl) apple cider vinegar

1 cup (2 dl) chicken stock

1 to 2 yellow onions, sliced

2 cloves garlic, sliced

3 tablespoons (½ dl) raisins

1 to 2 tablespoons of chipotle en adobo or chipotle paste

Salt

3 to 4 teaspoons arrowroot or cornstarch

In a pan, bring all of the ingredients to a simmer, covered, for 5 to 10 minutes. Add extra salt to taste. Add starch dissolved in 4½ tablespoons (¾ dl) cold water, to thicken. Serve the chutney lukewarm or room temperature.

GOOSEBERRY HABANERO CHUTNEY
Serves 4 to 6

Mackerel, salmon, and other oily fish pair very well with the fruity acid from the gooseberry and the agreeable pungency of the habanero.

1 quart (½ liter) half-ripe gooseberries

1 yellow onion, chopped

2 cloves garlic, coarsely chopped

2 fresh habanero chiles, seeded and thinly sliced, or 3 to 4 tablespoons habanero hot sauce

1 cup (2 dl) chicken stock

6 (1 dl) tablespoons sugar

1½ tablespoons (¼ dl) apple cider vinegar

Salt

3 to 4 teaspoons arrowroot or cornstarch

In a pan, bring all the ingredients to a slow simmer, covered, for 5 to 10 minutes. Add starch dissolved in 4½ teaspoons (¾ dl) of cold water, to thicken. Serve the chutney lukewarm or at room temperature.

Authentic Texan barbecue

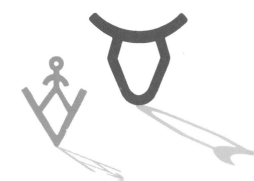

Barbecue is defined, first and foremost, as slow cooking over hot coals to give food a smoky taste. Grilling, on the other hand, is quick cooking over high heat. Barbecuing, therefore, is not the same thing as grilling—neither is it simply basting with a sauce. However, barbecue sauces and glazes do taste delightful on grilled food or served on the side.

To succeed in barbecuing, you need a good barbecue grill with a lid or a hood. Wood from deciduous, broad-leafed trees are preferable since they give a long-lasting heat and a better smoky flavor. Use briquettes or charcoal for those items which require shorter cooking time (e.g., fish, shellfish, or vegetables). Large pieces of meat or whole poultry, however, demand real wood.

Using tongs, put the food on the grill when the coals have a glowing ash-gray surface. Cover with the lid so the ingredients absorb the smoke and can finish cooking, as in an oven. Add barbecue sauce or glaze with a brush frequently, at regular intervals, during the cooking time. Barbecue sauce and glaze, as noted above, may be served on the side.

If you don't have access to a grill, there are a few tricks you can use to achieve equally successful results. Meat from the front of the animal, like the ribs and brisket of beef, can be cooked with spices and vegetables before it is grilled in the oven (see page 126). This way the meat is given extra flavor and a tender consistency. The smoky taste comes from liquid smoke, which is added while the meat is cooking. A smoke box is also a good alternative. Smoke boxes and smoking chips can be found in specialty kitchen stores. The box is primarily meant for fish, but works just as well on smaller pieces of meat or poultry. The smoke box can be used both on the stove or in the oven.

With a homemade barbecue sauce or glaze, you can really enhance the flavor of your food. Why not challenge your neighbors and friends to a barbecue cook-off— it may be the highlight of the year! Barbecue sauce and glaze can be made in advance; both keep well in the refrigerator or freezer. In the refrigerator, they keep for approximately a month, and in the freezer, for several months.

Glaze differs from barbecue sauce in that glaze is always transparent and has a shiny surface. However, both barbecue sauce and glaze serve the same purpose: They both infuse meat and fish with a wonderful flavor!

ANCHO BARBECUE SAUCE
—

One of my favorite sauces, this recipe has a dark, hot, sweet flavor with a touch of cocoa and coffee. Brush on chicken, pork, and game.

1 yellow onion, finely chopped

1 clove garlic, finely chopped

Corn or canola oil

6 tablespoons (1 dl) sugar

3 tablespoons (½ dl) apple cider vinegar

3 ancho chiles, presoaked in water and seeded

1¼ cups (3 dl) water from the presoaked anchos

5 cloves allspice, ground in a mortar

1 bay leaf

1 teaspoon instant coffee

3 tablespoons (½ dl) soy sauce

In a pan, sauté the onion and garlic in a little oil until soft. Add the other ingredients and let simmer over medium heat for approximately 30 minutes. Process until smooth.

DATE BARBECUE SAUCE
—

Dates have a ripe fruity taste with a rich, heavy, almost burnt sweetness. Brush this sauce on game, chicken, and pork.

1 yellow onion, finely chopped

1 clove garlic, finely chopped

Canola oil

20 dates, pitted

1¼ cups (3 dl) chicken stock

3 tablespoons (½ dl) apple cider vinegar

1 teaspoon sambal oelek or other hot sauce

3 tablespoons (½ dl) soy sauce

In a pan, sauté the onion and garlic in a little oil until soft. Add the rest of the ingredients and simmer over medium heat for 20 minutes. Process until smooth.

WHISKEY-CORN BARBECUE SAUCE
—

Rich with the sweetness of vegetables and the hot and smoky flavors of chipotle and whiskey—this is the All-American sauce. I like it best brushed on beef and entrecôte, and even on veal, chicken, and game.

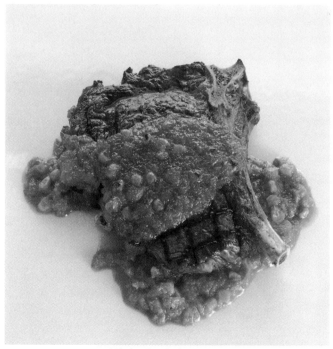

Whiskey-Corn Barbecue Sauce

2 cups (4 to 5 dl) fresh
corn kernels

3 to 4 shallots, finely
chopped

2 cloves garlic, finely
chopped

Canola oil

1/2 cup (3/4 dl) raw sugar
or brown sugar

3 tablespoons (1/2 dl)
apple cider vinegar

1 1/4 cups (3 dl) chicken
stock

Salt

2 teaspoons chipotle
paste, chipotle en
adobe, or dried chipotle

3 tablespoons (1/2 dl)
whiskey

In a pan, sauté the corn, shallots,
and garlic in a little oil until soft.
Add sugar, vinegar, and stock.
Bring to a boil. Season with salt
and chipotle. Continue to simmer,
covered, for 10 to 15 minutes.
Pour sauce into a food processor,
add the whisky, and mix to a
smooth sauce.

CHIPOTLE-PEANUT
BARBECUE SAUCE
—

Lightly smoked and hot. Brush
on game, beef, and poultry.

2 yellow onions,
chopped

2 cloves garlic, chopped

Peanut oil

4 1/2 tablespoons (3/4 dl)
brown sugar

3 tablespoons (1/2 dl)
apple cider vinegar

1 1/4 cups (3 dl) chicken
stock

2 to 3 tablespoons chipo-
tle en adobo, chipotle
paste, or dried chipotle

1/2 teaspoon ground
cinnamon

2 teaspoons instant
coffee

1 tablespoon peanut
butter

Sauté the onion and garlic in the
peanut oil until soft. Add the sugar, vinegar, stock, and chipotle.
Simmer, covered, for 10 to 15
minutes. Process until smooth.
Stir in cinnamon, instant coffee,
and peanut butter.

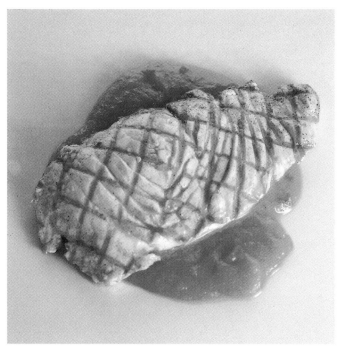
Apricot-Habanero Barbecue Sauce

APRICOT-HABANERO BARBECUE SAUCE

—

A fruity sweetness, a rich vegetable aroma, and a dash of habanero makes this sauce just perfect for salmon, halibut, and catfish. Try this with poultry or pork too.

> *1 yellow onion, finely chopped*
>
> *2 cloves garlic*
>
> *Corn or canola oil*

1 yellow bell pepper, roasted, peeled, and seeded

⅔ cup (150 g) dried apricots

1 ½ tablespoons (½ dl) apple cider vinegar

3 tablespoons (½ dl) brown sugar

1 ¼ cups (3 dl) water

1 tablespoon Coleman's powdered mustard

4 tablespoons habanero hot sauce

Salt

In a pan, sauté the onion and garlic in a little oil until soft. Add the remaining ingredients, except the mustard powder and habanero. Simmer, covered, for 20 minutes, or until the apricots are soft. Pour into a food processor. Season with mustard powder, habanero, and salt while processing to a smooth sauce.

TIGER BARBECUE GLAZE

—

A hot, sweet n' sour glaze—great with just about everything.

3 ounces (1 dl) sugar

3 tablespoons (½ dl) apple cider vinegar

1¼ cups (3 dl) chicken stock

1 yellow onion, finely chopped

1 clove garlic, finely chopped

3 to 4 red Dutch or Thai chiles, finely chopped

1 tablespoon honey

Salt

1 to 2 tablespoons arrowroot or cornstarch

Tiger Barbecue Glaze

Melt the sugar in a saucepan. Add the vinegar and chicken stock and bring to a boil. Add the onion, garlic, and chile. Simmer on low heat for 15 minutes. Add the honey and season to taste with salt. Add starch, which has been dissolved in 6 tablespoons (1 dl) cold water, to thicken until smooth. The glaze is now ready to use!

POMEGRANATE GLAZE
—

Brush this glaze on oily fish, or on crispy-fried duck, chicken, or turkey.

> 1 pomegranate, peeled, with juice and seeds
>
> 1 tablespoon honey
>
> 3 tablespoons (½ dl) apple cider vinegar
>
> ¾ cup (2 dl) chicken stock
>
> ½ teaspoon sambal oelek or hot sauce
>
> Salt
>
> 2 to 3 teaspoons arrow-root or cornstarch

Bring the pomegranate, honey, vinegar, and chicken stock to a boil. Season with sambal oelek and salt and let simmer for 5 minutes. Add starch, which has been dissolved in 3 tablespoons cold water, to thicken.

HONEY-TAMARIND GLAZE
—

The tamarind enhances the glaze with its exciting, somewhat sour plum taste. Great with fried or grilled pork, chicken, or game.

> ¾ cup (2 dl) chicken stock
>
> 1 yellow onion, finely chopped
>
> 1 teaspoon honey
>
> 1 teaspoon concentrated tamarind paste
>
> ½ teaspoon sambal oelek or hot sauce
>
> Salt
>
> 2 to 3 teaspoons arrow-root or cornstarch

In a saucepan, bring the chicken stock, onion, honey, and tamarind to a boil. Season with sambal oelek and salt and allow to simmer for 5 minutes. Add starch, which has been dissolved in 3 tablespoons water.

GINGER GLAZE
—

This popular glaze can be served with salmon and shellfish, or with chicken, pork, or vegetable dishes.

71

¾ cup (2 dl) sugar

3 tablespoons (½ dl) apple cider vinegar

1 ¼ cups (3 dl) chicken stock

1 ½ tablespoons (50 g) fresh ginger, peeled and thinly sliced

1 clove garlic, peeled and thinly sliced

1 tablespoon red Dutch chile, thinly sliced

1 to 2 tablespoons arrow-root or cornstarch

½ star fruit, thinly sliced

Salt

¼ to ½ cup (1 dl) sugar

3 tablespoons (½ dl) apple cider vinegar

1⅔ cup (4 dl) chicken stock

1 yellow onion, finely chopped

1 clove garlic, finely chopped

¾ cup (2 dl) black currants, puréed

1 to 2 tablespoons red Dutch chile, thinly sliced

½ teaspoon salt

2 to 3 teaspoons arrow-root or cornstarch

3 tablespoons (½ dl) Absolut Kurrant vodka

Melt the sugar in a saucepan. Add the vinegar and chicken stock. Bring to a boil and add the ginger, garlic, and chile. Let simmer for approximately 20 minutes. Season with salt. Add starch dissolved in about ⅓ cup (1 dl) water, to thicken. Place the slices of star fruit in the glaze or use to garnish.

Melt the sugar in a saucepan. Add the vinegar and chicken stock. Bring to a boil and skim. Add the onion, garlic, purée, chile, and salt. Simmer for approximately 20 minutes. Add starch dissolved in 3 tablespoons (½ dl) cold water to thicken. Last, but not least, flavor with Absolut Kurrant.

BLACK CURRANT GLAZE
—

These wonderful berries can be put to good use in a glaze which is excellent with roasted fowl, or as a spicy preserve to accompany meatballs and potato dumplings.

MAPLE SYRUP GLAZE

1/4 to 1/2 cup (1 dl) maple syrup

2 tablespoons rice vinegar

1/2 teaspoon sambal oelek or hot sauce

Salt

1 to 2 teaspoons arrowroot or cornstarch

In a pan, bring the maple syrup, vinegar, and sambal oelek to a boil. Season with salt. Thicken with starch dissolved in 3 tablespoons (1/2 dl) cold water.

LEMONGRASS GLAZE

4 1/2 tablespoons (3/4 dl) sugar

3 tablespoons (1/2 dl) rice vinegar

1 1/4 cups (3 dl) chicken stock

3 stalks lemongrass, thinly sliced

1 tablespoon red Dutch chile, thinly sliced

1 clove garlic, thinly sliced or chopped

Zest of 1 lime

1 to 2 tablespoons arrowroot or cornstarch

In a pan, melt the sugar. Add the vinegar and chicken stock. Skim and add the lemongrass, chile, garlic, and zest. Simmer for 10 to 15 minutes and thicken with starch dissolved in 6 tablespoons (1 dl) cold water.

LINGONBERRY KETCHUP

The children's favorite new ketchup, perhaps? Serve with everything from mashed potatoes to game.

1 1/4 cups (3 dl) fresh or frozen lingonberries

1 yellow onion, finely chopped

6 tablespoons (1 dl) sugar

1 3/4 cups (2 dl) water

2 green Dutch chiles, seeded and finely chopped, or 1 to 2 teaspoons sambal oelek

Put all the ingredients in a saucepan and simmer for 5 to 8 minutes, covered, over medium heat. Process until smooth. Allow to cool and pour into a bottle, which should be kept in the refrigerator.

MINT SAMBAL

Excellent as a mild condiment or in lamb casserole.

1 yellow onion, finely chopped

1 clove garlic, finely chopped

Canola oil

1²⁄₃ cups (4 dl) fresh mint leaves, packed

2 large green Thai chiles

3 tablespoons (¹⁄₂ dl) rice vinegar

Salt

Sauté the onion and garlic in a little oil until soft. Set aside and let cool. Blend remaining ingredients together in a food processor until smooth and season with salt. Store in a jar with a lid. Sambal will keep for about two weeks in the refrigerator.

CILANTRO SAMBAL
—

A great compliment to fish and shellfish soup, or as a seasoning for ground beef.

1 yellow onion, finely chopped

1 clove of garlic, finely chopped

Canola oil

1²⁄₃ cup (4 dl) fresh cilantro leaves

2 fresh jalapeño chiles or 3 tablespoons pickled jalapeño

3 tablespoons (¹⁄₂ dl) rice vinegar

Salt

Sauté the onion and garlic in a little oil until soft. Set aside and let cool. Process with remaining ingredients until smooth and season with salt. Store in a jar with a lid. Sambal will keep for about two weeks in the refrigerator.

COCONUT SAMBAL
—

In this recipe, the coconut comes into its own by balancing the mildly acidic taste of the lime. Use in casseroles, soups, and sauces when you are in the mood for something with a tropical taste!

1 yellow onion, finely chopped

2 cloves garlic, finely chopped

1 red Dutch chile, sliced

²⁄₃ cup (1 dl) coconut flakes

²⁄₃ cup (1 dl) water

Juice of 1 lime

Salt

Corn or canola oil

In a pan, sauté the onion and garlic in a little oil until soft. Add the chile, coconut flakes, and water. Bring to a boil, remove from heat, and let stand, covered, for 25 minutes so liquid can be absorbed. Purée the boiled coconut mixture with the lime juice until smooth and season with salt. Store, covered, in the refrigerator. Sambal will keep for approximately 2 weeks.

PASILLA-PLUM MOLE

—

My variation of this national Mexican sauce is particularly good with fried chicken, turkey, pork, and game.

1 yellow onion, coarsely chopped

1 clove garlic, chopped

Canola oil

¾ cup (2 dl) prunes, pitted

2 dried pasilla or ancho chiles

3 tablespoons (½ dl) balsamic vinegar

1¼ cups (3 dl) chicken stock

1 teaspoon chipotle paste or chipotle en adobo

2 to 3 tablespoons Ibarra chocolate

3 tablespoons strong coffee

1 tablespoon peanut butter

Salt

In a pan, sauté the onion and garlic in a little oil until soft. Add the prunes, chiles, vinegar, chicken stock, and chipotle. Simmer for 25 minutes.

Add the remaining ingredients. Process to a smooth sauce and season with salt. Dilute with more stock if the sauce is too thick.

POBLANO COMPOTE

—

1 yellow onion, finely chopped

2 cloves garlic, finely chopped

Corn oil

2½ cups (6 dl) chicken stock

1 cup (200 g) prunes, pitted

1 to 2 ancho chiles, pre-soaked, seeded, and puréed

3 tablespoons (½ dl) apple cider vinegar

Salt and freshly ground black pepper

In a pan, sauté the onion and garlic in a little oil until soft. Add the chicken stock, prunes, purée and vinegar. Simmer over low heat for approximately 25 to 30 minutes or until smooth and well-thickened. Season with salt and pepper.

JALAPEÑO-CHEESE DIP
Serves 4 to 6
—

1 yellow onion, finely chopped

1 clove garlic, finely chopped

2 tablespoons butter

2 tablespoons flour

2 cups (5 dl) warm milk

1 bay leaf

Pinch ground nutmeg

2 tablespoons pickled jalapeño, finely chopped

1 red bell pepper, roasted, peeled, and seeded

1 yellow bell pepper, roasted, peeled, and seeded

1 green onion, sliced

1⅔ cups (4 dl) grated cheddar cheese

Salt and freshly ground black pepper

In a pan, sauté the garlic in butter until soft. Add flour and stir well. Add the milk and beat into sauce until smooth and creamy. Stir in the bay leaf, nutmeg, and jalapeño. Season with salt and pepper. Simmer on low heat and stir frequently to avoid lumps or burning. Meanwhile, dice the bell pepper. Remove dip from heat and stir in the bell pepper, green onion, and cheese. Serve with warm corn tortilla chips.

HORSERADISH SAUCE
Serves 4
—

This zesty sauce is traditionally served with oysters in New Orleans, but is excellent with other types of shellfish and fish.

⅜ cup (1 dl) tomato ketchup

1 tablespoon habanero hot sauce

3 tablespoons fresh horseradish, grated

2 tablespoons freshly squeezed lemon juice

*¹/₂ teaspoon Worcester-
shire sauce*

Stir all the ingredients together
and serve. Will keep for a week in
the refrigerator.

PACIFIC PESTO
Serves 4 to 6
—

This recipe has been greatly
influenced by traditional Italian pesto. Try with wok-fried
noodles and vegetables or as a
topping for pizza.

> *1 to 2 large Thai or
> green Dutch chiles,
> seeded*
>
> *6 cloves garlic, roasted
> and peeled*
>
> *3 tablespoons (40 g)
> fresh ginger, peeled*
>
> *2 to 3 stalks lemongrass,
> sliced*
>
> *²/₃ cup unsalted peanuts*
>
> *1¹/₄ cups (3 dl) chopped
> fresh cilantro*
>
> *6 tablespoons (1 dl) pea-
> nut oil*
>
> *6 tablespoons (1 dl)
> fresh parmesan cheese,
> grated*

Purée all the ingredients together
until smooth. Store the pesto,
covered, in the refrigerator.

ROUILLE
Serves 4 to 6
—

Rouille is traditionally served
with Mediterranean bouilla-
baisse (fish soup). It is an excellent dipping sauce.

> *1²/₃ cups (4 dl) mayon-
> naise*
>
> *3 cloves garlic, peeled*
>
> *3 tablespoons (¹/₂ dl)
> tomato purée*
>
> *3 tablespoons (¹/₂ dl)
> sambal oelek*

Purée all the ingredients together
until smooth. Make a day in advance so the flavor can develop.

CHIPOTLE MUSTARD
—

Try with sausage and ham!

> *2 tablespoons Coleman's
> mustard powder*
>
> *2 tablespoons water*
>
> *2 tablespoons dark corn
> syrup*
>
> *1 to 2 tablespoons chipo-
> tle paste or chipotle en
> adobo*

In a jar, mix the mustard powder
with the water. Stir in the syrup
and chipotle. Store the mustard,
covered, in the refrigerator. It
will keep for approximately a
week.

AJVAR
—

1 yellow onion, finely chopped

2 cloves garlic, finely chopped

1 eggplant, peeled and cut in small pieces

Olive oil

2 to 3 fresh red Hungarian sweet or red bell peppers, roasted, peeled, and seeded

2 red Dutch chiles, roasted, peeled, and seeded

3 tablespoons apple cider vinegar

Salt

In a pan, sauté the onion, garlic, and eggplant in the oil until soft. Let cool. Purée with remaining ingredients until a smooth paste.

Season with salt. Store, covered, in the refrigerator. Ajvar will keep for approximately 2 weeks.

GUACAMOLE
Serves 4
—

2 large avocados

1 yellow onion, finely chopped

1 clove garlic, roasted, peeled, and crushed

Juice of ½ lemon or 1 lime

3 tablespoons olive oil

Salt

Scoop out the contents of two avocados and, using a fork, mix together with the other ingredients. Season with salt. Serve with warm corn tortilla chips.

Tip: to keep the guacamole from darkening, cover with thin slices of lemon.

Also try flavoring guacamole with these other ingredients:

finely chopped jalapeño or serrano chiles

1 tomato, cubed

Fresh cilantro, finely
chopped

½ cucumber, peeled and
cubed

1 stalk celery, cubed

½ papaya, cubed

1 orange, chopped

1 cup pineapple,
coarsely chopped

SEAFOOD STOCK
—

Homemade stocks are always good to have near at hand.

2 yellow onions, finely
chopped

3 cloves garlic, finely
chopped

2 carrots, finely
chopped

3 stalks celery, finely
chopped

Corn oil

1 pound (½ kilo) shrimp
or lobster shells,
crushed

1 bay leaf

1 teaspoon thyme

1 teaspoon ground cay-
enne pepper

Cold water

1 cup (2 dl) white wine

Sauté the vegetables in a little oil until soft—but without browning them. Add the crushed shells and stir. Then add the spices and cover with cold water and white wine if desired. Skim well. Let simmer on low heat for 4 hours. Strain the stock through a finely meshed strainer, and refrigerate or freeze for later use.

CHICKEN STOCK
—

Kill two birds with one stone by using the carcass from the chicken you've cooked for dinner.

Leftovers of 1 chicken
(cooked) or 1 fresh
chicken

2 yellow onions, coarsely
chopped

2 cloves garlic, crushed

2 carrots, coarsely
grated

Corn oil

10 black peppercorns,
coarsely ground

2 bay leaves

1 teaspoon thyme

1 small chile, dried and
finely shredded

In a pot, sauté the chicken leftovers and vegetables in a little oil. Cover generously with cold water and add the spices. Bring to a boil, slowly. Skim well and simmer on low heat for 6 to 10 hours. Pour the stock through a finely meshed strainer and refrigerate.

A simple tip is to let the broth or stock simmer overnight on the lowest possible heat. When you wake up in the morning, the stock is ready!

HOT CHILE OIL
—

This hot oil can be enjoyed in an endless variety of dishes. Brush it on meat, fish, shellfish, or poultry when roasting or grilling; use it to flavor breads, marinades, dressings, salsas; or sprinkle on freshly baked pizza.

1 quart (1 liter) canola oil

⅓ cup Thai, cayenne, ancho, or chipotle chiles, crushed and dried

Stir together the chile and oil in a saucepan. Warm slowly for 10 to 15 minutes. The oil must never be so hot that it begins to smoke. Pour into a suitable container and store in refrigerator for two weeks before straining. Store the oil in a glass bottle or decanter into which you have also added a whole dried chile to enhance the flavor.

Sharp Little Appetizers

GRILLED BRUSCHETTAS WITH BARBECUE SAUCE
Serves 4

Bruschettas can be eaten as an appetizer or cut into small pieces and served as a snack.

4 thick slices French bread

Ancho Barbecue Sauce or Chipotle-Peanut Barbecue Sauce (see pages 66 and 68)

Guacamole (see page 78)

Brush each bread slice on both sides with barbecue sauce. Grill them on both sides over red-hot glowing charcoal, or under the grill in the oven. Top with a generous helping of guacamole. Serve immediately!

CORN BRIOCHE MUFFINS WITH BLACK BEAN-MANGO-PROSCIUTTO-CHIPOTLE SALAD
Serves 4

This dish is suitable as an appetizer, a snack with cocktails, or as part of a buffet. You can also make the salad separately and serve it with warm tortillas.

Corn Brioche Muffins (see page 150)

4 ounces (100 g) prosciutto, diced
½ ripe mango, diced
½ cup (100 g) black beans, cooked
2 to 3 green onions, thinly sliced
1 teaspoon chipotle paste or chipotle en adobo
Salt

Begin by preparing the muffins. You can also reheat frozen brioche muffins.

In a bowl, mix together the prosciutto, mango, beans, and green onions and season with chipotle and salt. Cut off the top of each corn brioche, reserving them as lids, and hollow out the insides. Fill with salad and top with lids.

BASIC CEVICHE
Serves 4

Ceviche is a traditional Mexican seafood dish. The seafood is spiced raw (e.g., marinated in lime juice). Serve this dish in soup plates together with warm tortilla chips.

7 ounces (200 g) sea scallops or halibut, diced
1 avocado, diced
3 green onions, sliced
1 plum tomato, diced
2 cloves garlic, roasted, peeled, and crushed
2 tablespoons fresh jalapeño or serrano chile
Juice of 1 lime
1 bunch fresh cilantro, finely chopped
Salt

In a bowl, marinate the scallops or fish in the lime for 1 hour, stirring occasionally. Prepare the rest of the ingredients during this time.

Add remaining ingredients to the seafood and season with salt. Let stand in a cool place or in the refrigerator before serving.

SCALLOP CEVICHE IN PHYLLO TART
Serves 6

Scallops marinated in lime with serrano chiles and cilantro are the perfect accompaniment to a cold glass of beer or wine during cocktail hour.

Ceviche:

12 scallops, diced
½ cup (1 dl) freshly squeezed lime juice
1 ripe mango, diced
1 roasted red bell pepper, peeled, seeded, and diced
1 roasted yellow bell pepper, peeled, seeded, and diced
1 clove garlic, roasted, seeded, and crushed
3 green onions, thinly sliced
2 fresh serrano chiles, chopped
1 small bunch fresh cilantro, finely chopped
2 to 3 tablespoons olive oil
Salt

In a bowl, marinate the diced scallops in the lime for one hour. In the meantime, prepare the remaining ingredients.
Add the remaining ingredients to the scallops. Season with salt and lime.

Phyllo tart:

4 round pieces frozen phyllo pastry (approximately
3 inches in diameter) per person

Preheat the oven to 400 degrees. Layer the phyllo pastry pieces, one on top of the other. Brush the top layer with olive oil and salt. Bake in oven for 5 minutes. Rotate tart a quarter turn and bake for 3 more minutes. Serve the ceviche on the phyllo tart.

SALMON-GINGER MINT CEVICHE
Serves 4

---

7 ounces (200 g) salmon fillet, diced
3 tablespoons (40 g) fresh ginger, grated
3 to 4 stalks fresh mint, with leaves shredded
1 small piece fresh cucumber, diced
A small piece fresh pineapple, diced
3 green onions, sliced
2 cloves garlic, roasted, peeled, and crushed
1 large red Thai chile, seeded, and finely chopped
Juice of 1 lime
Salt

In a bowl, mix all the ingredients together and season with salt. Let the ceviche stand in a cold place for at least 15 minutes before serving, so the flavor has time to develop. Serve with warm tortilla chips.

Mayans prepare a meal on the beach.

LEMONGRASS CEVICHE
Serves 4

7 ounces (200 g) halibut fillet, diced in small cubes

3½ ounces (100 g) fresh shrimp, shelled

½ mango, diced in small cubes

2 to 3 stalks lemongrass, sliced very thin

3 green onions, sliced

2 cloves garlic, roasted, peeled, and crushed

*1 fresh habanero chile, seeded and finely chopped,
or 1 to 2 tablespoons habanero hot sauce*

Juice of 1 lime

Salt

In a bowl, mix all the ingredients together and season to taste. Let stand in a cold place for at least 15 minutes. Serve with warm tortilla chips.

GINGER CARAMEL HERRING
Serves 4

Herring and chiles? Of course! The rich flavor of herring is excellent with both chile and ginger.

½ cup (1¼ dl) sugar

⅔ cup (1½ dl) water

½ cup (1 dl) rice wine vinegar

*3 tablespoons (50 g) fresh ginger, peeled
and finely shredded*

1 tablespoon red Dutch chile, thinly sliced

2 to 3 salty herring fillets, which have been soaked well

1 baby leek, thinly sliced

Melt the sugar in a non-stick saucepan. Remove from heat and add the water and vinegar. Return to low heat. Add the ginger and chile, and let mixture slowly come to a boil. Remove from heat immediately and let cool.

Cut the herring fillets into 1 inch (2 to 3 cm) thick pieces and, alternating with the leek, stir into the completely cooled sugar mixture. Marinate the herring fillets for at least 24 hours before serving.

LEMONGRASS HERRING
Serves 4

A Thai-inspired marinade with a fresh flavor.

½ cup (1 dl) rice wine vinegar

½ cup (1¼ dl) sugar

⅔ cup (1½ dl) water

3 stalks lemongrass, thinly sliced

3 lime leaves

*1 tablespoon large red Thai chile, thinly sliced,
or 10 dried piri piri, crushed in a mortar*

*2 to 3 large salty herring fillets, which have
been soaked well*

In a saucepan, bring the vinegar, sugar, water, lemongrass, lime leaves, and chile to a boil. Let cool.

Cut the herring fillets into 1 inch (2 to 3 cm) thick pieces and stir them into the completely cooled mixture. Marinate the herring fillets for at least 24 hours before serving.

LINGONBERRY-HABANERO HERRING
Serves 6

⅔ cup (1½ dl) water

½ cup (1 dl) plus 2 tablespoons sugar

½ cup (1 dl) apple cider vinegar

*1 cup (2 dl) lingonberries (or cranberries),
fresh or frozen*

*1 to 2 fresh habanero chiles, seeded and thinly sliced,
or 2 to 3 tablespoons habanero hot sauce*

*2 to 3 large salty herring fillets, which have
been soaked in water*

1 red onion, cut into thin rings

*1 Gravenstein apple (or any eating apple),
cored and sliced*

Garnish with:

1 red onion, cut into thin rings

1 apple, cored and sliced

In a saucepan, bring the water, sugar, vinegar, lingonberries (or
cranberries), and chile to a boil. Allow to cool. Cut the herring fillets
into 1 inch pieces (2 to 3 cm) and place these in layers in the cooled
mixture with red onion and apple. Marinate the herring fillets for at
least 24 hours. When serving, garnish the herring with more onion
rings and apple slices.

HOUSE SMOKED SALMON WITH TOMATILLO-AVOCADO SALSA
Serves 4

You will need a smoke-box (see page 65) for this sensational appetizer (it's worth every penny!). Arugula's spicy flavor is a
wonderful complement to both salmon and avocado.

*4 salmon fillets, 3½ ounces (100 g) each, scaled but
with the skin left on*

Salt

2 handfuls arugula

Tomatillo-Avocado Salsa (see page 50)

Preheat oven to 350 (175C) degrees.
    Prepare the smoke-box according to directions. Place the salmon fil-
lets in the box for 7 minutes. Put the box in the oven for 4 to 5 minutes.
Serve the salmon immediately on a bed of arugula and top with salsa.

MUSSELS WITH
SPICY GREMOLATA CROUTONS
Serves 4

2¼ pounds (1 kg) fresh mussels
6 shallots or 1 large onion, finely chopped
2 cloves garlic, finely chopped
1 yellow or red bell pepper, diced in tiny cubes
Olive oil
1 small bunch of parsley, chopped
½ cup (1 dl) white wine
1 cup (2 dl) water
Salt

Clean the mussels by scraping them with the back of a knife. Pull the beards off with a knife or tong and then rinse them in cold water. Discard mussels that won't close when you tap them with the knife.

In a large pan, sauté the shallots or onion, garlic, and bell pepper in a little oil until soft. Add the mussels, wine, and water and cover with a lid. Let the mussels simmer a minute or two, or until they open. Season with salt. Sprinkle the chopped parsley over the mussels and serve them with warm gremolata croutons.

Gremolata croutons:

3½ ounces (100 g) butter, softened to
room temperature
Zest of 1 lemon
3 cloves garlic
1 small bunch parsley
1 to 2 tablespoons pickled jalapeño chile
6 slices French bread

Preheat oven to 400 (200C) degrees.

Process the butter with the lemon peel, garlic cloves, parsley, and jalapeño until smooth. Spread the butter on the bread slices. Cut them diagonally and toast them in the oven for 6 to 7 minutes.

Mussels with Spicy Gremolata Croutons

GOAT CHEESE CHILE RELLENO
Serves 4

A modern variation of a Southwestern classic.

½ yellow onion, finely chopped

1 clove garlic, finely chopped

1 small piece celery, finely diced

3 tablespoons (½ dl) pine nuts

Corn or canola oil

*4 green chiles (Hungarian Wax, New Mexican,
Anaheim or Poblano), roasted, peeled,
and seeded*

2½ ounces (75 g) goat cheese

2 ounces (50 g) mozzarella

**Pear-Cashew Nut Salsa or Salsa Fresca
(see page 51 or 52)**

In a pan, sauté the onion, garlic, celery, and pine nuts in a little oil. Let cool. In a bowl, mix sautéed vegetables really well with the cheeses. Fill the chiles with the cheese mixture.

Goat Cheese
Chile Relleno

Batter:

1 egg, with the yolk and the white separated
½ cup (1 dl) corn flour
Salt

In a bowl, whisk the egg yolk together with 1 to 2 tablespoons corn flour. Whisk the egg white until stiff and carefully fold into the corn flour and yolk mixture. Heat ¼-inch of oil in frying pan until hot but not smoking. Dip the stuffed peppers in the batter and then in the rest of the corn flour so that they are completely covered. Fry in oil until golden brown. Let drain on paper towels. Lightly season with salt. Serve the peppers on a bed of Salsa Fresca or Pear-Cashew Nut Salsa.

GOAT CHEESE
AND PEAR QUESADILLA
Serves 4

A Mexican snack with a fruity new twist. Serve as a snack or appetizer.

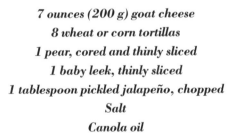

7 ounces (200 g) goat cheese
8 wheat or corn tortillas
1 pear, cored and thinly sliced
1 baby leek, thinly sliced
1 tablespoon pickled jalapeño, chopped
Salt
Canola oil

Spread goat cheese on each tortilla. Then place the pear, leek, and jalapeño equally on top of the cheese and sprinkle with salt. Place the other 4 tortillas on top, like a sandwich.

Fry each quesadilla in a little oil on both sides on low heat until the cheese melts. Cut the quesadillas in quarters and serve.

Wild Mushroom-Mozzarella Quesadilla

WILD MUSHROOM-MOZZARELLA QUESADILLA
Serves 6

1 1/2 cups (3 g) wild mushrooms, chopped
1 yellow onion, finely chopped
1 clove garlic, finely chopped
Olive oil
Salt and freshly ground black pepper
1 to 2 teaspoons chipotle paste or chipotle en adobo
1 bunch parsley, chopped
1/2 cup (100 g) mozzarella cheese, in thin slices
8 wheat or corn tortillas

In a pan, sauté the mushrooms, onion, and garlic in a little oil. Season with salt and pepper. Set aside the mushrooms and add the chipotle and parsley. Distribute the mozzarella on 4 tortillas and then spread the mushroom mixture over it. Place the remaining tortillas on top, like a sandwich.

Sauté each quesadilla on both sides in a little oil over low heat until the cheese melts. Serve the quesadillas cut into pieces with a crisp salad.

SPICY LIMA BEANS
Serves 4 to 6

An excellent hors d'oeuvres which can be served by itself, with sliced tomatoes and fresh home-baked bread, or as an accompaniment to fish, chicken, and pork. This dish should be prepared when fresh broad beans are available.

1 pound (500 g) large dried white beans, soaked
overnight in water, or fresh broad beans

Marinade:

1/2 cup (1 dl) extra virgin olive oil
3 tablespoons (1/2 dl) apple cider vinegar

3 cloves garlic, roasted, peeled, and crushed
1 tablespoon finely chopped jalapeño or serrano chile
2 tablespoons Dijon mustard
2 teaspoons ground cumin
Salt and freshly ground black pepper
6 tablespoons (1 dl) finely chopped fresh
parsley, basil, or cilantro

In a pot, boil the beans in salted water, covered, for 35 to 45 minutes, or until they are soft.

In the meantime, make the marinade. In the bowl of a food processor, purée all the ingredients for the marinade until smooth. Season to taste and pour into a large bowl.

When the beans are soft, drain and let the steam evaporate for several minutes. Then stir in the marinade. Marinate for at least two hours, but preferably overnight in the refrigerator. Sprinkle a little freshly chopped herb over the beans before serving, to garnish.

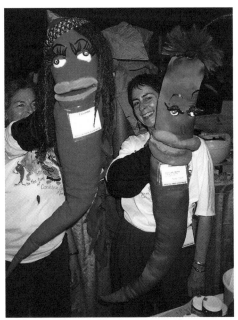

Happy and hot at the Fiery Food Show in Albuquerque

TURKEY TOSTADA SALAD

Crisp salad with grilled turkey breast and warm corn tortillas

Serves 4 to 6

Tortilla chips, warm

1 head romaine lettuce, coarsely shredded

3 tomatoes, in quarters

8 green onions, sliced

4 eggs, hard boiled and in slices

3½ ounces (100 g) cheddar cheese, coarsely grated

20 jalapeño chiles, mild or strong

½ cup (1 dl) sour cream

Guacamole (see page 78)

1 pound (500 g) turkey breast in slices

Salt and freshly ground pepper

Roasted Red Pepper Salsa (see page 54)

Prepare all the ingredients. Place the warm tortilla chips on a large salad plate. Cover with some of the salad, tomatoes, green onions, eggs, cheese, chiles, sour cream, and guacamole. Repeat, layer by layer, until you have a delightful large salad.

Sauté or grill the slices of turkey. Season with salt and freshly ground black pepper. Place the slices around the salad and, using a spoon, drizzle the Red Pepper Salsa over the whole salad.

GARDEN TORTILLAS ENCHILADAS
Serves 4

Enchiladas means "flavored with chile" in Spanish. This is a "green kitchen" variation.

2 yellow onions, finely chopped

1 clove garlic, finely chopped

1 red bell pepper, diced

1 yellow bell pepper, diced

1 stalk celery, diced

Olive oil

1 (16-ounce) can crushed tomatoes

Pinch cumin

1 (16-ounce) can red kidney beans, rinsed and well drained

4 wheat or corn tortillas

3½ ounces (100 g) grated cheese

Hot sauce, your favorite

Sour cream, guacamole, lettuce, and red onion to garnish

In a pan, sauté the onions, garlic, bell peppers, and celery in a little oil until soft. Add the tomatoes and cumin. Simmer slowly, covered, for 20 minutes. Add the kidney beans and simmer for 10 more minutes.

In a pan, warm tortillas quickly in a little oil on both sides. Let them drain on paper towels and brush both sides with hot sauce. Top each one with the bean mixture.

Preheat oven to 350 (175C) degrees.

Roll up each tortilla, place in an ovenproof dish, sprinkle with grated cheese, and bake in oven for approximately 10 minutes.

Garnish with suggested ingredients.

CHILE CON FRIJOLES
Serves 4 to 6

A rich and nourishing three-bean chili served with sour cream, guacamole, red onion, and warm corn tortillas. Also tastes great served with grilled chicken, beef, and pork.

1 yellow onion, finely chopped

2 cloves garlic, finely chopped

1 stalk celery, diced

Corn oil

2½ cups (6 dl) chicken stock

1 tablespoon chili powder

1 tablespoon chipotle paste or chipotle en adobo

1 teaspoon ground cumin

1 cup (2 dl) black beans, pre-soaked and boiled

1 cup (2 dl) pinto beans

1 cup (2 dl) red kidney beans, pre-soaked and boiled

Salt

1 red bell pepper, roasted, peeled, seeded, and diced

1 tablespoon oregano

1 to tablespoons corn flour (optional)

In a pot, sauté the onion, garlic, and celery in a little oil until soft. Add the chicken stock and all the spices except the oregano. Let simmer, covered, for approximately 20 minutes. Add the cooked beans and simmer for 10 more minutes. Add salt to taste. Add the diced bell pepper and crumbled oregano. For a smoother consistency, thicken with corn flour, mixed together with 6 tablespoons (1 dl) cold water.

ROASTED PEPPER PIZZA
Serves 4 to 6

This is a real family pizza!

Pizza dough:

1 ounce (25 g) yeast

1 cup (2½ dl) warm water

½ teaspoon salt

Pinch sugar

2½ cups (325 g) unbleached wheat flour plus flour for rolling out the dough

3 tablespoons olive oil

2 zucchinis, sliced and grilled or sautéed until soft

1 onion, sliced, and grilled or sautéed until soft

2 red bell peppers, roasted, peeled, and seeded

2 yellow bell peppers, roasted, peeled, and seeded

2 cloves garlic, roasted, peeled, and crushed

3½ ounces (100 g) fresh parmesan cheese, grated

3½ ounces (100 g) mozzarella, grated or sliced

3½ ounces (100 g) Fontina cheese, grated

Salt and freshly ground black pepper

Fresh oregano

Preheat the oven to 450 (230C) degrees.

Make the pizza dough in a bowl or in a food processor. Dissolve the yeast in the warm water. Add the salt and sugar and work the flour in gradually until the dough becomes elastic. Knead the dough for 15 minutes by hand, or 5 minutes in the bowl of a heavy-duty mixer.

Put the dough in a clean bowl with 1 tablespoon olive oil. Turn the dough around in the oil so that the surface of the dough will not get dry. Allow the dough to rise for 1 hour under a moist towel. In the meantime, prepare the vegetables and cheeses.

Place the dough on a well-floured surface and roll it out so that it will fit on a baking sheet. Mix the garlic with the rest of the olive oil and brush over the dough. Distribute a little of the parmesan cheese over

99

the dough and place the vegetables on top. Season with salt and pepper and sprinkle the rest of the cheese on the vegetables.

Bake the pizza in the oven for 12 to 18 minutes. Chop some fresh oregano and sprinkle on top before serving.

MAPLE-GLAZED GARDEN SALAD
Serves 4

3 Jerusalem artichokes, scrubbed and cut in half

2 parsnips, peeled and cut in half, lengthwise

3 carrots, peeled and cut in half, lengthwise

3 onions, cut in quarters

½ celeriac, peeled and cut into cubes

8 leaves Chinese cabbage or bok choy (Note: You can find bok choy in most Asian supermarkets. It's a cabbage with long white stems and light green leaves.)

Salt and freshly ground black pepper

Roasted sesame seeds

Roasted peanuts

Canola oil

Maple Syrup Glaze (see page 73)

Boil each root vegetable separately, until soft. Spread them out in an ovenproof dish, drizzle with oil, and season with salt and pepper.

Grill the root vegetables or broil them in the oven. Brush them with the glaze. In a hot pan, sauté the cabbage quickly in some oil and serve as a bed for the root vegetables. Garnish with sesame seeds and peanuts. Serve immediately!

WILD MUSHROOM PASTA
Serves 4

1½ pounds (600 g) mixed wild mushrooms,
washed and sliced

1 yellow onion, finely chopped

2 cloves garlic, finely chopped

Olive oil

Salt and freshly ground black pepper

2½ cups (6 dl) chicken stock

3 tablespoons (½ dl) balsamic vinegar

1 teaspoon chipotle paste or chipotle en adobo

14 ounces (400 g) fettucini pasta

3 tomatoes, diced

2 green onions, sliced

Freshly grated parmesan cheese

In a wide pan, sauté the mushrooms, onion, and garlic in some oil. Add salt and pepper and then add the chicken stock, vinegar, and chipotle. Bring to a boil. In the meantime, in a pot, boil the pasta in lightly salted water. When it is almost done, drain and add to the mushrooms. The pasta will continue cooking in the stock, and infuse it with a taste of mushrooms, onion, and spices.

Remove the pan from the heat and stir in the diced tomatoes and green onions. Serve immediately with freshly grated parmesan.

WOK-FRIED SALAD
Serves 4

Get out your wok or your biggest frying pan.

9 ounces (250 g) spiral pasta, cooked

1 carrot, sliced thinly

5 ounces (150 g) mushrooms, cut in half

1 red bell pepper, seeded and thinly sliced

1 yellow bell pepper, seeded and thinly sliced

½ zucchini, thinly sliced

1 baby leek, cut diagonally

Peanut oil

Salt and freshly ground black pepper

¼ head (100 g) green cabbage, cut in thick strips

⅔ cup (150 g) fresh bean sprouts

Tiger Barbecue Glaze or Ginger Glaze (see page 70 or 71)

1 bunch fresh cilantro, chopped

Toasted sesame seeds, onion, or peanuts to garnish

Prepare glaze and set aside.

Heat a wok or a large frying pan with some peanut oil. Add the pasta, carrot, mushrooms, bell peppers, zucchini, and leek. Stir continuously. Season with salt and pepper. Add cabbage and bean sprouts and continue stirring. Add Tiger Barbecue Glaze or Ginger Glaze to taste. Serve salad immediately with cilantro sprigs and sesame seeds or other garnish.

HELL IN TEXAS

(ANONYMOUS)

THE DEVIL IN HADES WE'RE TOLD WAS CHAINED,
AND THERE FOR A THOUSAND YEARS REMAINED.
HE DID NOT GRUMBLE NOR DID HE GROAN,
BUT DETERMINED TO MAKE A HELL OF HIS OWN
WHERE HE COULD TORTURE THE SOULS OF MEN
WITHOUT BEING CHAINED IN THAT POISONED PEN

SO HE ASKED THE LORD IF HE HAD ON HAND
ANYTHING LEFT WHEN HE MADE THE LAND
THE LORD SAID ,"YES, I HAVE LOTS ON HAND,
BUT I LEFT IT DOWN BY THE RIO GRAND."

SO THE DEVIL WENT DOWN AND LOOKED AT THE STUFF.
AND SAID IF IT COMES AS A GIFT HE'D BE STUCK
FOR AFTER EXAMINING IT CARFULLY AND WELL,
HE FOUND IT TOO DRY FOR HELL.

SO IN ORDER TO GET IT OFF'N HIS HANDS
THE LORD PROMISED SATAN HE'D WATER THE LANDS,
FOR HE HAD SOME WATER, OR RATHER SOME DREGS,
THAT SMELLED LIKE A CASE OF BAD EGGS.

SO THE DEAL WAS MADE AND THE DEED WAS GIVEN
AND THE LORD WENT BACK TO HIS HOME IN HEAVEN.
"NOW, SAYS THE DEVEIL, "I HAVE ALL THAT'S NEEDED
TO MAKE A GOOD HELL, AND HE DAMN WELL SUCCEEDED

HE PUT THORNS ON THE CACTUS AND HORNS ON THE TOADS
AND SCATTERED TARRANTULAS ALONG THE ROADS.
HE GAVE SPIRAL SPRINGS TO THE BRONCO STEED
AND A THOUSAND LEGS TO THE CENTIPEDE

AND HE GREW THE RED PEPPERS THAT GROW BY THE BROOKS-
THAT THE MEXICANS USE WHENEVER THEY COOK
JUST DINE WITH THEM ONCE- YOU'LL BE SURE TO SHOUT
FROM HELL ON THE INSIDE AS WELL AS OUT.

EGGS IN HELL
Serves 4

Two things inspired this dish: Jeremiah Tower's cookbook, *New American Classics*, and the classic Mexican egg dish, huevos rancheros. Enjoy—and let yourself be inspired by eggs in hell!

½ leek, sliced
¼ cup (50 g) butter
12 eggs, lightly beaten
1 to 2 tablespoons fresh or pickled jalapeño, sliced
Salt and freshly ground black pepper
1 small bunch fresh cilantro, chopped
8 wheat tortillas
1 avocado, sliced
½ head romaine lettuce, coarsely shredded
New Mexican Red Chile Salsa (see page 56)

In a pan, sauté the leek in butter until soft. Lower the heat. Stir in the eggs and jalapeño. Add salt and pepper to taste. Stir, using a wooden spoon, until the egg mix has thickened, yet is still smooth and creamy. Sprinkle cilantro on top and serve immediately with hot tortillas, avocado, lettuce, and New Mexican Red Chile Salsa.

JALAPEÑO CHEESE OMELETTE
Serves 4

3 yellow onions, sliced
Canola oil
9 ounces (250 g) smoked ham, in strips
2 tablespoons fresh or pickled jalapeño
½ cup (100 g) feta cheese, diced
10 to 12 eggs, lightly beaten
1 small bunch fresh cilantro or parsley, chopped
Salt

In a pan, sauté the onion in a little oil until soft. Add the ham, chile, and cheese to the eggs and stir gently. Add salt to taste. On medium heat, pour the egg mixture in the pan with the onions. Stir with a fork and shake pan occasionally.

Continue cooking on low heat until omelette feels firm to the touch. Sprinkle freshly chopped cilantro on top and serve directly from the pan.

GINGER-GLAZED SALMON
Serves 4

Get ready for one of the world's best salmon dishes. This classic combination of flavors is celebrated on both sides of the Atlantic with much success.

Ginger Glaze (see page 71)
4 to 5 ounces each (150 g) salmon fillets, with skin left on
Corn oil
Salt and freshly ground black pepper
1 pound (400 g) potatoes, cooked and sliced
1 baby leek, thinly sliced
8 leaves green Chinese cabbage
Butter
Toasted sesame seeds
Parsley leaves for garnish

Preheat oven to 400 (200C) degrees. Prepare Ginger Glaze and set aside. Rub fillets with a little oil and salt. Lay them in a baking pan with skin side up and bake in oven for 6 to 7 minutes.

In a wide pan, gently sauté potatoes, leek, and Chinese cabbage in a little butter until lightly browned. Season to taste with salt and pepper. Remove from heat and transfer to serving dish. Place fillets on top of vegetables and drizzle generously with glaze. Sprinkle with sesame seeds and garnish with parsley.

Ginger-Glazed Salmon

Grilled Swordfish with Two Salsas and Corn Strips

GRILLED SWORDFISH WITH
TWO SALSAS AND CORN STRIPS
Serves 4

Swordfish, salmon, and tuna are fatty fishes, best served when done medium, whereas halibut is best well-done. Today, swordfish can be found in most fish markets.

Black Bean-Corn-Cilantro Salsa (see page 54)
Tomatillo-Avocado Salsa (see page 50)

8 corn or wheat tortillas, cut in 1/2-inch wide strips and sautéed in corn oil until crisp

4 to 5 ounces each (150 g) swordfish, salmon, tuna, or halibut steaks
Canola oil
Salt and freshly ground black pepper

Prepare the two salsas and set aside. You can also prepare the tortillas in advance and then heat them in the oven before serving. Brush the fish steaks with some oil and grill or fry them for 2 to 3 minutes on each side. Add salt and pepper to taste. Wrap the steaks in aluminum foil and let them rest for a minute. Serve the fish on the Black Bean Salsa. Top with Tomatillo Salsa and tortilla strips.

FISH SOUP WITH ROUILLE
Serves 4 to 6

This soup is inexpensive and easy to make. Add lobster, shrimp, crayfish, or mussels to make it even more festive. Serve with toasted croutons and grated gruyère cheese.

1 1/2 to 2 pounds (600 to 700 g) cod or ling fillet, cut in small pieces

2 to 3 yellow onions, coarsely chopped
3 to 4 carrots, sliced
2 to 3 stalks celery, sliced
1 bulb fennel, thinly sliced
3 cloves garlic, finely chopped
Canola oil
1 quart Shellfish Broth (see page 79)
2 tablespoons ground fennel seed
2 bay leaves
2 tablespoons ground paprika
4 to 5 medium-sized potatoes, sliced
Fresh parsley or dill to garnish
Salt

Rouille (see page 77)

In a pan, sauté all the vegetables, apart from the potatoes, in oil until they are soft. Add the broth and slowly bring to a boil. Skim carefully and then add the spices. Let simmer, covered, for 20 to 25 minutes. Add the potato slices and continue simmering until the potatoes are quite soft. Add fish and simmer again until the fish is completely cooked, about 15 to 20 minutes.

Chop parsley or dill or both and add to soup. Ready to serve!

WHOLE ROASTED WOLFFISH WITH LOBSTER-ORANGE SALSA
Serves 4 to 6

A whole fish is both festive and impressive served to guests, especially if it's the awesome and terrifying wolffish.

1 whole wolffish, catfish or lake bass, 3½ to 4½ pounds (1½ to 2 kg)
Salt

Marinade:

Scant ½ cup (2 dl) sugar
Juice of 1 lemon, plus zest

Juice of 1 orange, plus zest
Juice of 1 lime, plus zest
1 tablespoon red Dutch chile, thinly sliced
2 cloves garlic, thinly sliced
Salt and freshly ground pepper
2 to 3 teaspoons (10 to 15 ml) arrowroot or cornstarch

Lobster-Orange Salsa (see page 53)

In a pan, melt the sugar and then stir in the citrus juices, the chile, and the garlic. Season with salt and pepper and stir in starch mixed with 3 tablespoons of cold water to thicken. Remove marinade from heat and cool. Then add the fish and let marinate for at least 3 hours. Turn the fish in the marinade a couple of times.

Prepare grill or preheat oven to 350 degrees (175C).

Grill, or roast the fish in the oven for 25 to 35 minutes. Baste the fish with the marinade every 5 minutes. Sprinkle fish with salt just before serving.

Whole Roasted Wolffish with Lobster-Orange Salsa

CARIBBEAN RICE WITH RED BEANS AND GARLIC-CHILE MUSSELS
Serves 4

Green mussels from the Pacific Ocean are sometimes sold under the name "New Zealand green mussels." You'll find them in most well-stocked fish markets.

1¼ cup (3 dl) rice

1 yellow onion, finely chopped

1 clove garlic, finely chopped

Corn oil

2 tablespoons curry powder

Scant 1 cup (2 dl) grated fresh coconut, soaked in 2 cups (5 dl) of warm water

2 cups canned red kidney beans, well rinsed and drained

1 piece fresh pineapple, diced

Salt

Mussels:

24 green mussels

⅔ cups (1½ dl) of corn oil

1 clove garlic, minced

2 teaspoons sambal oelek or hot sauce

1 small bunch green onions, thinly sliced

1 to 2 tablespoons soy sauce

Boil the rice first and set aside. In a pan, sauté the onion and garlic in a small amount of oil until soft. Add curry. Stir and sauté gently on low heat. Add the rice, grated coconut in its water, beans, and pineapple. Add salt to taste. Simmer gently on low heat for about 20 minutes.

In the meantime, prepare the mussels. Preheat oven to 350 degrees. Beat the oil, garlic, sambal, onions, and soy sauce together. Put the mussels in an ovenproof dish and pour the sauce over them. Bake for 6 to 7 minutes. Serve on a big plate with the rice in the middle and the mussels around the edge.

DUCK SURPRISE

Roasted duck with orange and rice

Serves 4

Anyone who has seen "Fawlty Towers" with John Cleese knows what a Duck Surprise is. Here is my homage to this classic television series.

1 fresh duck, 5½ to 6½ pounds (2½ to 3 kilos)

2 tablespoons ground orange zest

*1 tablespoon ground jalapeño or
1 to 2 teaspoons cayenne*

Salt

1⅔ cups (4 dl) rice

3 whole star anise

3 eggs

1 baby leek, cut in narrow strips

½ red bell pepper, diced

½ yellow bell pepper, diced
Salt and freshly ground black pepper
Canola oil

Roasted Garlic and Mango Chutney (see page 61)

Preheat oven to 350 (175C) degrees.

Cut off the wings of the duck and save the innards. These can be used to make your own stock (see page 79). Dry the duck with paper towels and rub the spices on the inside and outside of duck. Rub the skin with lots of zest and salt to make it nice and crispy.

Put the duck with its back facing up on a rack in an ovenproof dish. Roast in oven and turn after 1 hour. Roast for another hour with the breast facing up. While the duck is roasting, spray it lightly 2 to 3 times with ice water to make it extra crispy.

Boil the rice in advance with the anise. Set aside to cool. Heat a frying pan or wok with some oil right before serving. Fry the eggs, stirring continuously with a wooden spoon. Stir in the leek, peppers, and anise-flavored rice. Sauté for another minute or two while stirring. Add spices to taste. Put the rice on a large serving plate and place the duck on top. Carve the duck at the table and serve with Roasted Garlic and Mango Chutney.

CHICKEN AND SEAFOOD GUMBO
WITH POTATO SALAD
Serves 4

Play a rhythm and blues CD for inspiration while making this soulful dish.

5 ounces (150 g) bacon, shredded
7 ounces (200 g) spicy sausage, thinly sliced
7 ounces (200 g) chicken breast, cut into small pieces
3 to 4 yellow onions, finely chopped
3 cloves garlic, finely chopped
1 large yellow bell pepper, diced
1 large red bell pepper, diced
5 to 6 stalks celery, finely chopped
3½ ounces (100 g) okra, sliced

1 tablespoon chili powder

1 (16-ounce) can crushed tomatoes

¼ cup (¾ dl) rice

1 quart (1 liter) Seafood Stock or Chicken Stock
(see page 79)

2 bay leaves

1 teaspoon thyme

3 teaspoons oregano

Freshly ground black pepper

Sambal oelek or hot sauce

7 ounces (2 dl) wheat flour

Salt

11 ounces (300 g) shelled crayfish tails or 1½ pound
(½ kg) whole crayfish with tails shelled,
but left on the body

In a big pot over medium heat, sauté the bacon, sausage, and chicken. Add all the vegetables except the okra, and the chili powder. Stir frequently for about 5 minutes.

Add tomato, rice, and broth. Bring to a boil. Lower heat and let simmer for 1 hour. Skim the fat and reserve in an iron skillet. Add the spices and the okra last, once all the fat has been skimmed.

Heat the fat in the skillet and stir in the flour. Stir continuously until the flour has turned brown. Be careful, it can easily burn and stick. This is called making a *roux*, a brown thickening, and will give the soup a distinct flavor.

Whisk in some of the roux to the soup until you are happy with the soup's consistency. Add salt to taste and add the crayfish. Mix tails and whole crayfish, if possible. Serve in deep plates with potato salad.

Potato salad:

4 medium-sized potatoes, boiled, peeled, and diced

6 hard-boiled eggs, finely chopped

6 green onions, thinly sliced

1 stalk celery, finely diced

1 small red bell pepper, finely diced

2 tablespoons Dijon mustard
Scant ½ cup (1 dl) mayonnaise
Scant ½ cup (1 dl) sour cream
Salt and freshly ground black pepper

Mix all the ingredients in a big bowl. Add salt and pepper to taste and let stand in a cold place until the gumbo is ready.

POLLO POBLANO
Serves 4

Poblano Compote (see page 75)

4 large chicken drumsticks
Salt and freshly ground black pepper

Peanut oil
1 cup (200 g) spiral pasta, cooked
1 red bell pepper, seeded and shredded
1 yellow bell pepper, seeded and shredded
1 carrot, thinly sliced
1 baby leek, sliced diagonally
⅔ cup (150 g) mushrooms, sliced in half
½ zucchini, thinly sliced
Salt and freshly ground black pepper

Prepare grill or preheat oven to 350 (175C) degrees.
   Prepare Poblano Compote and set aside.
   Grill the drumsticks or bake in oven for 30 to 35 minutes. Heat a wok or a large frying pan. Add some peanut oil and then the pasta with the vegetables. Stir-fry for 2 minutes, stirring continuously. Add salt and pepper to taste. Serve with Poblano Compote over the warm pasta.

HABANERO-LIME CHICKEN WITH SWEET GARDEN RICE
Serves 4 to 6

1 fresh chicken, 3½ pounds (1½ kilos),
in serving-size pieces

2 to 3 yellow onions, quartered

2 cloves garlic, finely chopped

3 carrots, sliced thickly

3 stalks celery, sliced

Canola oil

¼ teaspoon salt

2 bay leaves

Zest of 2 limes plus juice

1 fresh habanero chile, seeded and sliced thinly
or habanero hot sauce

2 egg yolks

1 to 2 tablespoons arrowroot or cornstarch

Sweet Garden Rice:

1⅔ cups (4 dl) long-grain rice

Salt

3 tablespoons golden raisins

1 piece carrot, finely diced

1 baby leek, green part only, finely diced

1 red bell pepper, finely diced

Scant ½ cup (1 dl) roasted peanuts or almonds

In a large pan, sauté the chicken, onion, garlic, carrots, and celery
with a little oil. Add water just to cover. Add salt and bring to a boil
slowly. Skim and then add bay leaves, lime zest, and habanero. Let
simmer, covered, for 15 to 20 minutes.

Pour out at least half of the broth and refrigerate or freeze for another use. Carefully combine the lime juice, egg yolks, and starch and
then pour into the pan with the chicken and the vegetables while stirring with a large wooden spoon. Add salt to taste. Let the sauce thicken
before serving.

While the chicken is simmering, prepare the rice. Bring salted water to a boil, then add raisins and carrot cubes. When the water comes to a boil again, add the rice and simmer on low heat, covered. When the rice is done, stir in the leek, pepper, and nuts.

NORTH-OF-THE-BORDER CHICKEN WITH PASILLA-PLUM MOLE
Serves 6

This is my interpretation of modern Southwestern cuisine. The chicken is glazed with pomegranates, chiles, and honey and is served with small corn tamales filled with chorizo sausage.

Pomegranate Glaze (see page 71)
Pasilla-Plum Mole (see page 75)

1 fresh whole chicken, 4½ pounds (2 kilos)
Salt and freshly ground black pepper

Tamales:

Dried or fresh corn husks, soaked in warm water
1 cup (2 dl) fresh corn kernels
2 yellow onions, finely chopped
2 cloves garlic, finely chopped
1 egg
1 cup (2 dl) corn flour
1 teaspoon baking powder
3½ ounces (100 g) smoked ham or
bacon in strips
2 to 3 small chorizo sausages, thickly sliced
Corn oil

Preheat oven to 350 (175C) degrees. Start by making the glaze and the mole. Set aside.

Rub the chicken inside and out with salt and season with freshly ground black pepper. Roast for 1 hour and 40 minutes in the oven. During the last 40 minutes, baste the chicken with the glaze every 5 minutes.

Make the tamales while the chicken is roasting in the oven. Sauté half the corn, 1 onion and 1 garlic clove in some oil until lightly browned. Let the vegetables cool and then purée them in a blender. Mix together the purée, eggs, corn flour, and baking powder in a bowl to make a light dough and put aside. Dry the corn husks.

Using a knife or a pair of scissors, cut each husk to make 2 strips to tie the tamale together. Spread out 2 leaves so that the long sides are parallel to each other. Let them overlap by about 2 to 3 inches. Put a spoonful of the dough in the middle of each leaf. Make sure there is a piece of sausage in each tamale. Roll them lengthwise to make a bundle. Tie them at each end, using the strips the way a party firecracker is tied together.

Plan for 2 to 3 tamales per person. Steam the tamales in a Chinese bamboo basket for 20 minutes. If you don't have a bamboo baskets or a steamer, you can put the tamales in a big colander and fit the colander into a big saucepan with a tight-fitting lid.

North-of-the-Border Chicken with Pasilla-Plum Mole

117

SPICY SMOKED BREAST OF CHICKEN
Serves 4

A smoke box is required for this robust recipe.

Ancho Barbecue Sauce (see page 61)
Corn-Green-Onion-Tomato Salsa (see page 55)

8 corn or wheat tortillas, cut into
¼-inch-thick strips and sautéed in
corn oil until crispy

4 chicken breasts
Salt
3 star anise, dried
2 cinnamon sticks
4 cloves
3 tablespoons mustard seeds
3 tablespoons coriander seeds
2 tablespoons cumin seeds
2 tablespoons allspice seeds
Scant ½ cup (1 dl) smoke chips

Make the barbecue sauce, salsa, and tortilla strips first.

Season the chicken breasts with salt and keep them at room temperature for 20 minutes.

Preheat oven to 350 (175C) degrees. Use a mortar and pestle to crush the seeds and mix them with the smoke chips. Put the chicken and the seasoned chips in the smoke box on a hot stove. Let chicken smoke for 15 to 20 minutes. Then place in hot oven for 15 to 20 minutes.

Take the chicken breasts out of the smoke box and make sure they are done. Brush each breast with barbecue sauce and serve them on plates surrounded by the salsa. Pile corn strips like a haystack on top.

SOUTHWESTERN CASSOULET
Serves 4 to 6

Cassoulet is a good example of a terrific, everyday dish whose ingredients lend color, flavor, and consistency to a nourishing meal—a "one dish meal." The chicken can be exchanged for lamb, pork, beef, or game. Make a double batch and put half in the freezer.

1 chicken, 3½ pounds (1½ kilos), cut into four pieces
9 ounces (250 g) salted pork or bacon, cut into strips
12 to 15 shallots
2 cloves garlic, chopped
2 to 3 carrots, sliced
2 to 3 stalks celery, sliced
3 to 3⅓ cups (7 to 8 dl) Chicken Stock (see page 79)
3 tablespoons (½ dl) balsamic vinegar
1⅓ cups (4 dl) cannellini beans or big white beans, soaked and parboiled
9 ounces (250 g) chorizo sausage, or other spicy sausage, sliced
12 to 15 sun-dried tomatoes, cut into strips
1 pinch thyme
2 bay leaves
3 tablespoons chopped fresh sage
1 to 2 teaspoons sambal oelek
Salt and freshly ground black pepper
2 to 3 tablespoons arrowroot or cornstarch

Brown the chicken and pork or bacon in a big pot. Lower the heat and add shallots, garlic, carrots, and celery. Sauté for five minutes. Add the stock, vinegar, sausage, beans, and sun-dried tomatoes. Bring to a slow boil. Skim and season.

Season with remaining spices. Let simmer, covered, for 40 to 45 minutes. Thicken using starch mixed in about ½ cup (1 dl) of cold water. Serve with crusty bread.

TERIYAKI CHICKEN WITH HOT POTATOES
Serves 4

1 pound (500 g) chicken parts, boned

1 yellow bell pepper, cut into large chunks

1 red bell pepper, cut into large chunks

1 yellow onion, cut into large chunks

8 bamboo skewers, soaked in water

1 (12-ounce) bottle teriyaki marinade

16 small potatoes, boiled

1 (14-ounce) can (380 g) pickled vegetables

1 tablespoon pickled jalapeño chiles, chopped

½ cup (1 dl) chopped parsley

Thread pieces of chicken, bell pepper, and onion onto each skewer and marinate for at least 1 hour, but preferably overnight. Turn the skewers in the marinade a couple of time.

Pan-fry or grill the skewers while making the hot potatoes. Heat the potatoes, pickled vegetables, and jalapeño in a saucepan with a lid. Remove from heat just as the vegetables are about to come to a simmer. Serve as a bed for the chicken skewers and decorate with parsley.

LAMBSHANK WITH WILD MUSHROOM
CHIPOTLE BARLEY RISOTTO
Serves 4

Ask your butcher to cut portion-sized pieces about 3 inches above the knuckle or use slices of shank or shoulder.

4 lamb shanks, 1 to 1½ pounds (500 to 600 g) each

3 yellow onions, coarsely chopped

3 cloves garlic, chopped

Corn oil

3 bay leaves

1 teaspoon thyme

1 teaspoon rosemary

*1 teaspoon black peppercorns, crushed with
a mortar and pestle*

Salt

Roasted Red Pepper Salsa (see page 54)

121

Chipotle Barley Risotto:

1½ cups (4 dl) barley

1 yellow onion, finely chopped

2 cloves garlic, finely chopped

1 carrot, finely diced

1 to 2 stalks celery, finely diced

1 cup (200 g) wild mushrooms, chopped

*1 to 2 teaspoons chipotle paste or
chipotle en adobo*

Corn oil

4 green onions, sliced

Salt

In a big pot, brown the lamb and vegetables in some oil. Cover with 3½ cups cold water and bring to a slow boil. Skim the broth carefully and then add remaining spices. The broth should be slightly salty to give the meat extra flavor. Cover the pot with a lid and let simmer for approximately 1 hour or until the meat is tender.

Make the barley risotto. In a smaller saucepan, sauté all the vegetables except the green onions in some oil. Ladle the broth from the lamb over the vegetables and add the barley and the chipotle. Cover with a lid.

Let the barley simmer according to instructions on the package. Season with salt and add the green onions right before serving to add color. Serve the lamb over the risotto and top with salsa.

COUSCOUS MY WAY
Serves 6 to 8

Make a big batch and freeze some for a future quick supper. This dish is great all year round.

4½ pounds (2 kilos) lamb shoulder, in slices or pieces

Olive oil

3 yellow onions, coarsely chopped

3 cloves garlic, finely chopped

2 carrots, coarsely chopped

2 red Dutch chiles, seeded and finely chopped

½ teaspoon thyme

½ teaspoon marjoram

2 bay leaves

1 teaspoon ground cumin

Salt and freshly ground pepper

*14 ounces (400 g) lamb sausage, fresh
or lightly smoked*

2 zucchinis, coarsely chopped

2 red bell peppers, roasted, peeled, and seeded

2 yellow bell peppers, roasted, peeled, and seeded

2 to 3 tablespoons arrowroot or cornstarch

In a big pot with a lid, brown the lamb with the onions, garlic, carrots, and chiles in a little oil. Cover with cold water and bring to a boil. Skim carefully and season with all the spices. Cover with lid and let simmer for about 1 hour.

Meanwhile, sauté the lamb sausages and add them to the pot along with zucchini and bell peppers in chunks. Remove about 2 cups (5 dl) of the broth to use for the couscous. Add starch dissolved in about ½ cup (1 dl) cold water to thicken remaining liquid.

Couscous:

1 small carrot, finely chopped

1 stalk celery

½ yellow onion, finely chopped

1 clove garlic, finely chopped

Olive oil

2 cups (5 dl) lamb broth, from above recipe

Salt and freshly ground black pepper

2 cups (350 g) couscous

In a pan, sauté the vegetables in some oil. Add the broth and bring to a boil. Season to taste with salt and pepper. Add the couscous and cover the pan with a lid. Let the couscous absorb the water on very low heat for about 5 minutes. Serve with the lamb on top.

CHILE-CHARGED LAMB MEATLOAF
Serves 4

1 to 2 yellow onions, finely chopped

1 to 2 carrots, finely chopped

Olive oil

1 cup (2½ dl) lamb broth or Chicken Stock
(see page 79)

Scant 1 cup (2 dl) green Anaheim chile flakes

1 tablespoon pickled jalapeño chiles, chopped

1½ pounds (600 g) ground lamb

1 egg

10 cloves garlic, roasted and peeled

3 tablespoons fresh sage, chopped

1 pinch grated nutmeg

Salt and freshly ground black pepper

1⅔ cup (4 dl) kritharaki (Greek durum pasta)

Corn-Green Onion-Tomato Salsa or Onion-Mint
Chutney (see page 55 or 60)

Preheat oven to 350 (175C) degrees.

In a pan, sauté the onions and carrots in some oil until soft. Add broth, chile flakes, and chile. Bring to a boil. Remove from heat and set aside to cool.

In a bowl, mix the lamb with the sautéed vegetables, egg, garlic, and spices. Fill a loaf pan with the mixture and bake in the oven for 45 minutes. In the meantime, boil the kritharaki in salted water.

Cut slices of the lamb meatloaf and serve over pasta with salsa or chutney.

MAPLE-ROASTED PORK WITH
GARLIC-GREEN CHILE MASHED POTATOES
Serves 4 to 6

*2¼ pounds (1 kg) lean salted pork or bacon,
in one piece with rind removed*

1 yellow onion, coarsely chopped

1 clove garlic, minced or chopped

2 carrots, thickly sliced

2 bay leaves

1 teaspoon thyme

10 allspice cloves, ground in mortar and pestle

5 piri piri, ground in mortar and pestle

Maple Syrup Glaze (see page 73)

Preheat oven to 350 (175C) degrees.

Put all the ingredients in a big pot. Cover with cold water and cover with lid. Bring to a slow boil. Skim and let simmer for 1½ hours. Remove from heat and let cool.

Lift the meat out of the broth and place in roasting pan. Strain the broth and freeze for later use. Then roast the meat in oven for 45 minutes. During the last 10 to 15 minutes, broil the meat and baste with maple syrup 4 to 5 times. You can also use your grill.

Carve the meat into ½-inch slices and serve with mashed potatoes.

Garlic-Green Chile Mashed Potatoes:

2 pounds (1 kg) potatoes

3 to 4 cloves garlic, peeled and chopped

3 ounces (50 g) butter

1 cup (2 dl) green chiles, chopped

1 cup (2 dl) Chicken Stock (see page 79) or milk, warm

1 baby leek, green part only, shredded

Salt and freshly ground black pepper

In a pot, boil the potatoes in salted water until soft. Drain water and let potatoes steam, covered. Sauté the garlic in 1 ounce of the butter and add it to the potatoes together with the chiles. Mash thoroughly.

Add broth or milk and remaining butter. Whisk until light and fluffy. Mix in leek and season to taste with salt and pepper.

BARBECUED RIBS

Serves 4

This dish should be prepared a day in advance, to allow the cooked pork to rest in its juices. I always strain the broth and refrigerate or freeze it to use at another time.

2¼ pounds thick pork ribs

2 yellow onions, coarsely chopped

2 cloves garlic, chopped

2 carrots, coarsely chopped

2 bay leaves

1 tablespoon black peppercorns, ground in mortar and pestle

1 tablespoon allspice cloves, ground in mortar and pestle

Scant ½ cup (2 dl) hickory or mesquite liquid smoke

Salt

4 potatoes

Tiger Barbecue Glaze or Ancho Barbecue Sauce (see page 70 or 66)

Preheat oven to 400 (200C) degrees.

Put the ribs, all the vegetables except the potatoes, and spices into a big pot. Add liquid smoke and cover with water. Bring to a slow boil, season with salt, cover, and let simmer for 1 hour. Add the potatoes and simmer for the last 20 minutes. Remove the pan from the heat and let the ribs and the potatoes cool in the broth, ideally overnight.

Meanwhile, make the glaze or the sauce and set aside. Lift out the ribs and potatoes and transfer to a cutting board. Cut the ribs into portion-size pieces along the bones and cut the potatoes into segments. Put the meat and potatoes on a baking sheet and broil for 15 to 20 minutes. You can also use your grill. Brush the ribs 4 to 5 times with the glaze or sauce while they are being grilled. Ready to serve with coleslaw.

Coleslaw:

3 tablespoons (½ dl) apple cider vinegar

1 egg yolk

1 to 2 tablespoons Dijon mustard

Barbecued Ribs

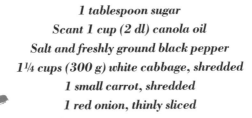

1 tablespoon sugar
Scant 1 cup (2 dl) canola oil
Salt and freshly ground black pepper
1¼ cups (300 g) white cabbage, shredded
1 small carrot, shredded
1 red onion, thinly sliced

Make the coleslaw while the ribs are simmering. In a bowl, mix together the vinegar, egg yolk, mustard, sugar, and oil. Season to taste with salt and pepper. Mix dressing with the vegetables in a larger bowl and refrigerate before serving.

BEEF BUDAPEST
Serves 4 to 6

Inspired by Hungarian cuisine, this dish is perfect on a cold and windy autumn or winter evening. Pork or chicken may be substituted. If you want a stronger flavor, I suggest adding some spicy sliced sausage. Serve this dish in deep plates with rice or sauerkraut.

4 yellow onions, chopped
2 cloves garlic, finely chopped
Canola oil
4 to 5 tablespoons ground paprika
2¼ pounds (1 kg) stewing beef, in small pieces
3 to 4 carrots, sliced
1 to 2 parsnips, sliced
2 bay leaves
Salt and freshly ground black pepper
4 to 6 potatoes, diced
1½ teaspoons caraway seeds
Fresh parsley, to garnish
4 red bell peppers, roasted, seeded, and peeled

In a pan, sauté the onion and garlic until soft, but not brown, in some oil. Stir in ground paprika, meat, carrots, parsnips, and bay leaves.

Season with salt and pepper and cover with cold water. Let simmer for 50 to 60 minutes on low heat and then skim carefully.

When 10 minutes remain, add diced potatoes and caraway seeds. Garnish with chopped parsley and diced peppers just before serving.

BARBECUED BEEF BRISKET WITH
NEW POTATOES IN SPICY CAESAR DRESSING
Serves 4 to 6

Prepare the beef one day in advance so that it can rest in its juices. If you want the characteristic smoky taste which is so typical of a barbecue, add some liquid smoke while simmering the beef. I always strain the broth and refrigerate or freeze it to use at a later time.

2¼ pounds (1 kg) brisket of beef

2 yellow onions, chopped

2 cloves garlic, chopped

2 carrots, chopped

2 bay leaves

1 tablespoon black peppercorns, ground in mortar and pestle

1 tablespoon allspice cloves, ground in mortar and pestle

Salt

1¾ pounds (800 g) new potatoes, scrubbed clean

Chipotle-Peanut Barbecue Sauce (see page 68)

Dressing:

2 egg yolks

1 to 2 cloves garlic

Juice of ½ lemon

2 teaspoon Dijon mustard

3 tablespoons anchovy fillet plus broth
1 to 2 tablespoons pickled jalapeño chiles
½ cup (1¼ dl) olive oil
1 cup (2 dl) grated parmesan cheese
Few sprigs parsley
Freshly ground black pepper

Prepare the grill.

Put the meat, all the vegetables except the potatoes, and spices in a big saucepan and cover with cold water over low heat. Let simmer, covered, for at least 2 hours or until the meat is tender. Skim regularly. Remove from heat and set aside to cool.

Prepare barbecue sauce and set aside.

Lift the meat out of the broth and transfer to grill. Brush the meat several times with the barbecue sauce. Carve into serving portions.

To make dressing, put all the ingredients except the oil and the parmesan cheese into a blender. Blend, adding oil and parmesan slowly, to make a creamy dressing. Season with black pepper. Boil the potatoes in salted water until done. Let them steam for awhile before mixing with the dressing. Serve the warm potato salad with the barbecued beef.

TEXAS CHILE CON CARNE
Serves 4 to 6

This classic dish was first sold by street vendors, the so-called "chili queens," of San Antonio, Texas. Since then, it's become a worldwide success!

1½ pounds (600 g) stewing beef, in small pieces
5 ounces (150 g) bacon, shredded
Canola oil
3 yellow onions, finely chopped
2 cloves garlic, finely chopped
2 red bell peppers, diced
2 bottles dark beer
2 tablespoons fresh or pickled jalapeño chiles,
finely chopped

1 tablespoon chipotle paste or chipotle en adobo

1 pinch ground cinnamon

1 teaspoon cumin

1 tablespoon oregano

Salt

In a pan over medium heat, brown the meat and bacon in some oil. Add onion, garlic, and bell pepper and sauté on low heat until the onion and bell pepper are soft. Add beer and bring to a slow boil. Skim carefully and then add the remaining ingredients except the oregano.

Simmer, covered, for 2 to 2½ hours, or until the meat almost falls apart. Add oregano during the last 10 to 15 minutes of cooking time. **Tip:** Serve with warm tortillas, grated cheddar cheese, chopped red onions, sour cream, guacamole, shredded iceberg lettuce, and rice.

ARCTIC WILD GAME CHILI
Serves 4 to 6

1½ pounds (600 g) ground venison

5 ounces (150 g) smoked ham or bacon, shredded

15 to 18 shallots

4 stalks celery, diced

2 cloves garlic, finely chopped

5 ounces (150 g) mixed wild mushrooms

1 cup (2½ dl) beef broth or Chicken Stock (see page 79)

Scant ½ cup (1 dl) balsamic vinegar

1 cup (2½ dl) dark beer

1 tablespoon ground ancho chile pepper

1 teaspoon ground cumin

2 tablespoons chipotle paste or chipotle en adobo

2 bay leaves

Salt

Canola oil

Apple-Lingonberry Salsa (see page 52)

In a pan, brown the venison, ham or bacon, and shallots with some oil. Add celery, garlic, and mushrooms and sauté for 5 minutes. Add broth, vinegar, and beer. Bring to a boil and skim. Add the spices, cover, and let simmer on a low heat for 35 minutes. Serve with salsa and warm tortillas.

JONAS'S CHILI-DOG
Serves 4

This is a sausage classic with cult status; the perfect midnight snack for chile lovers.

4 all-beef hot dogs, of best quality
1⅔ cups (4 dl) Texas Chile Con Carne (see page 130)
3½ ounces (100 g) grated cheese
4 tablespoons Guacamole (see page 78)
2 tablespoons pickled jalapeño chiles
4 mini-baguettes, split

Boil, fry, or grill the sausages, depending on your preference. Serve the sausages on baguettes topped with the chili, cheese, guacamole, and jalapeño (in that order). A real chili dog deluxe.

CHORIZO SANDWICH
Serves 4

Always great with a beer.

2 tablespoons anchovy fillet, chopped
2 to 3 chorizo sausages, sliced ⅓-inch thick
1 red onion, thinly sliced
2 tablespoons chopped fresh cilantro or parsley
1 tablespoons pickled jalapeño chiles
4 tablespoons extra virgin olive oil
4 mini-baguettes, split

Preheat the oven to 300 (150C) degrees.
    In a bowl, mix all the ingredients together and fill each baguette with the mixture. Heat sandwiches in oven for 10 minutes. Serve warm.

COUSCOUS-LAMB SAUSAGE
Serves 4

You can find sausage casing at your butcher or market hall. Serve the sausages with Muscat Grape Salsa and Spicy Lima Beans (see pages 54 and 93).

1 yellow onion, finely chopped

2 cloves garlic, finely chopped

1 small carrot, finely chopped

½ stalk celery, finely chopped

½ red bell pepper, finely chopped

Olive oil

3 cups (7 dl) lamb broth or Chicken Stock (see page 79)

⅔ cup (1½ dl) couscous

1½ pounds (600 g) lamb, ground coarsely

1 teaspoon ground paprika

1 teaspoon freshly ground black pepper

1 teaspoon ground cumin

*10 sprigs fresh thyme leaves, chopped, or
1 teaspoon dried thyme*

10 sprigs fresh sage, chopped, or 1 teaspoon dried sage

2 to 3 teaspoons sambal oelek or hot sauce

1 tablespoon salt

Sausage casing from sheep

In a pan, sauté the vegetables with some oil. Add 1 cup (2 dl) of the broth and season with spices, herbs, hot sauce, and salt. Bring to a boil. Pour in the couscous. Cover and let couscous absorb the water for 5 minutes on very low heat. Then pour the couscous into a wide pan to cool off quickly.

Mix the ground lamb with the cooled couscous and add the rest of the broth to make a moist filling. Fill the casing, using a pastry bag and tube, and let the sausage rest for 1 hour before frying or grilling.

JAMAICAN "JERK" CHICKEN SAUSAGE
WITH BURNING LOVE
Serves 4

"Jerk" is the name of a traditional spice marinade from the Caribbean which is primarily used for chicken and pork. You'll need a 2-pound (1 kilo) chicken if you want to debone it yourself. Use the leftovers to make Chicken Stock (see page 79).

1 to 2 yellow onions, finely chopped

2 cloves garlic, finely chopped

Canola oil

1 to 1½ pounds (500 to 600 g) ground chicken

2 teaspoons allspice cloves, ground in mortar and pestle

1 teaspoon freshly ground black pepper

1 pinch ground nutmeg

½ teaspoon ground cinnamon

1 tablespoon salt

8 sprigs fresh thyme or 1 teaspoon dried thyme

30 leaves fresh sage or 2 teaspoons dried sage

1 teaspoon brown sugar

*1 fresh habanero chile, seeded and finely chopped,
or 2 to 3 tablespoons habanero hot sauce*

Juice of 1 lime

1 tablespoon soy sauce

2 tablespoons (¼ dl) orange juice

Sausage casing from sheep

In a pan, sauté onions and garlic in some oil until soft. Cool and set aside.

Mix the chicken with all the spices, herbs, sugar, chile or hot sauce, onion, the lime juice, the soy, and the orange juice to make a smooth filling.

Fill the casing with the filling using a pastry bag and tube. Let the sausages rest for 1 hour before frying or grilling.

Burning Love:

2 pounds (1 kg) potatoes
9 ounces (250 g) bacon or smoked pork, shredded
1 to 2 yellow onions, chopped coarsely
1 fresh jalapeño or serrano chile, seeded, and
finely chopped
Scant 1 cup (2 dl) milk, warm
¼ cup (50 gr) butter
Chives, finely chopped, to garnish
Salt and freshly ground black pepper

Boil the potatoes until done. Drain water and set aside to steam. Meanwhile, fry the onions and bacon together until lightly browned. Add the chile to the potatoes and mash together in a saucepan. Add milk and butter. Whisk until fluffy. Finally, stir in onion, bacon, and top with chives. Season with salt and pepper before serving.

Almond-Fruit Cake with Dutch Chile Glaze, page 142
Ancho-Malt Syrup Torte, page 143
Cheesecake Caliente, page 144

Sweet & Hot Desserts with a Bite

The sweet and sour flavors of different fruits and berries, and the richness of nuts and chocolate, match the taste of chiles in a delightful way. In Mexico, you will often find street vendors selling fresh fruit powdered with ground chile. The hot flavor of ground chile pepper in desserts makes for a refreshing ending to every meal—guaranteed!

EXOTIC FRUIT & BERRY SOUP WITH STAR ANISE AND DUTCH CHILE
Serves 6
—

A dessert with lots of flavor, and inspired by Asia. Choose fruits and berries which are in season.

HOT AND SWEET FRUIT SALAD WITH LEMONGRASS AND THAI CHILE
Serves 4
—

1 quart (1 liter) freshly squeezed orange juice

1½ cups (3½ dl) sugar

4 star anise, dried

10 cloves, ground in mortar and pestle

1 tablespoon red Dutch chile, seeded and finely chopped

3 cups mixed fruit and berries, sliced (pineapple, mango, banana, grapes, strawberries work very well together)

Vanilla ice cream

1 cup (2 dl) of water

3 tablespoons (½ dl) sugar

2 stalks lemongrass, finely sliced

1 tablespoon red Thai chile, seeded and finely sliced

2 cups mixed fruit, sliced (mango, banana, papaya, pears, peaches, melon are wonderful)

Scant ½ cup (1 dl) fresh coconut, grated and roasted

Sorbet or ice cream

In a saucepan, simmer juice with the sugar. Skim carefully and add the spices and chile. Let simmer on low heat for 10 to 15 minutes. The juice mustn't boil!

Cool the consommé and add fruit and berries. Let stand 5 to 10 minutes before serving in a deep plate with a scoop of vanilla ice cream.

Boil the water, sugar, lemongrass, and chile in a saucepan. Let simmer for a minute. Cool. Add fruit and marinate in consommé for at least 1 hour. Serve in deep plates with grated coconut and sorbet or ice cream.

Hot and Sweet Fruit Salad with Lemongrass and Thai Chile

GINGER-PEACH CHILE PEARS
Serves 4

—

4 Anjou or Williams pears

1 to 1¼ cups (2 to 3 dl) sugar

Scant ½ cup (100 g) ginger, peeled and finely shredded

2 tablespoons red Dutch chile, finely sliced

2 bay leaves

1 quart (1 liter) water

Vanilla ice cream

Peel and core the pears. Slice each bottom so pears will stand upright. Put the pears and the other ingredients in a saucepan and cover with water. Let the pears simmer for 40 to 50 minutes or until soft. Cool. Serve the pears cold or warm with vanilla ice cream.

PASSION FRUIT MANGO COMPOTE WITH SERRANO CHILE AND ANISE-ALMOND COOKIES
Serves 4

—

10 passion fruits, pulp only

1 mango, coarsely chopped

Passion Fruit Mango Compote with Serrano Chile and Anise-Almond Cookies

Scant ½ cup (1 dl) sugar

1 fresh serrano chile, finely chopped

1 cup (2 dl) water

1 to 2 tablespoons arrowroot or cornstarch

In a saucepan, bring the passion fruit, mango, sugar, chile, and water to a slow boil. Let simmer on very low heat for 15 minutes. Thicken compote with starch diluted in 4½ tablespoons (¾ dl) water. Serve the compote lukewarm or cold with cookies on the side.

Cookies:

¾ cup (1¾ dl) sugar

3½ ounces (100 g) unsalted butter

1 teaspoon aniseed

1 egg

1¼ cup (3 dl) wheat flour

½ teaspoon double-action baking powder

Almond flakes

Preheat oven to 350 (175C) degrees.

In bowl of electric mixer or by hand, beat the sugar and butter until fluffy. Stir in aniseed and egg and keep mixing. Then add the flour and baking powder. Mix until smooth and refrigerate for 1 hour.

Roll out the dough to a thickness of about ¼ inch (0.6 cm) with a rolling pin on a floured surface. Cut out round cookies using a cookie cutter and place on a baking sheet lined with parchment paper. Top with the almond flakes and bake in the oven for 12 minutes.

Dunk the cookies in the compote to complete dessert.

COCONUT-JALAPEÑO PARFAIT WITH PINEAPPLE SALAD
Serves 4 to 6
—

A Caribbean-inspired dessert with a flavor reminiscent of the popular piña colada. The pineapple may be substituted with mango or papaya.

2 cups (5 dl) coconut milk

7 egg yolks

1½ cups (3 dl) sugar

1 to 2 tablespoons fresh jalapeño chile, seeded and finely chopped

3 tablespoons (½ dl) rum

1¼ cups (3 dl) cream

Pineapple salad:

1 fresh pineapple, cored and chopped

2 tablespoons confectioners' sugar

Juice of 1 lime

Hazelnuts, chopped

In a saucepan, whip the coconut milk, egg yolks, sugar, and chile together. Heat slowly until just before the mixture boils (180°F/82°C), which is the ideal temperature for the liquid to thicken. Remove from heat. Pour the mixture into a bowl and cool, using a water bath.

Add the rum to the mixture and stir. Whip the cream until soft peaks form. Carefully fold into mixture so that it does not lose its volume. Pour the parfait into a baking dish and freeze, preferably overnight.

Transfer parfait to refrigerator 25 to 30 minutes before serving to give it a soft consistency.

Mix the pineapple with the lime juice and the confectioners' sugar. Arrange the pineapple salad on plates. Place a slice of parfait on top of the salad and sprinkle some chopped hazelnuts to garnish.

ALMOND-FRUIT CAKE WITH DUTCH CHILE GLAZE
Serves 4 to 6
—

Almond crust:

4½ ounces (125 g) unsalted butter

⅔ cup (150 g) sugar

3 eggs

½ cup (90 g) ground or finely chopped almonds

1 bitter almond, ground

¼ cup (50 g) almond paste

4½ tablespoons (45 g) wheat flour

3½ ounces (100 g) mascarpone cheese, cream cheese, or plain yogurt

1½ to 2 cups pineapple, kiwi, mango, or strawberries, sliced

Glaze:

3 tablespoons (½ dl) sugar

Scant ½ cup (1 dl) water

1 tablespoon red or green Dutch chile, finely diced

1 to 2 teaspoons potato flour

Preheat oven to 350 (175C) degrees.

Start by making the crust. In the bowl of an electric mixer, beat butter and sugar until fluffy. Add the eggs one by one and whisk carefully after each one. Then add the remaining ingredients to make a smooth batter.

Pour the batter into a buttered baking dish (approximately 10 x 12 x 2) with parchment paper lining the bottom. Bake in the oven for 35 to 40 minutes. Check the crust by sticking a thin knife blade into it. When the knife comes out clean, the crust is ready. Let cool under a kitchen towel on a rack, which will keep it moist.

Spread the mascarpone on the crust evenly and spread the thinly sliced fruit on top.

For the glaze, melt the sugar in a saucepan to make a light caramel. Add water and chile and let simmer for 10 to 15 minutes. Add starch diluted in 1 ounce (¼ dl) cold water, to thicken. Set aside to cool. Glaze the fruit and then serve.

ANCHO-MALT SYRUP TORTE
Serves 8
—

Dough:

1½ heaping cups (3¾ dl) wheat flour

5 ounces (150 g) unsalted butter

2 tablespoons sugar

1 tablespoon cold water

Filling:

2 ancho chiles, dried, and soaked in warm water for 3 hours

5 eggs, lightly beaten

Scant 1 cup (2 dl) dark malt syrup

1 teaspoon vanilla

2½ ounces (75 g) unsalted butter, melted

Scant 1 cup (2 dl) roasted macadamia nuts, hazelnuts, walnuts, or pecans

Make the dough first since it needs to chill for 1 hour. In the bowl of an electric mixer, beat the flour, butter, and sugar. Add 1 tablespoon water and continue mixing until dough is smooth. Wrap the dough in plastic wrap and let it rest in the refrigerator.

Preheat oven to 350 (180C) degrees.

Butter and flour a tart pan with a removable base (12 inches [30 cm] in diameter). Roll out the dough with a rolling pin and press into tart pan. Cover with aluminum foil and fill with dried beans, peas, or rice to keep crust from bubbling. Bake the crust in the oven for 20 minutes. Remove the beans and the foil and cool on a rack.

In the bowl of an electric mixer, make a purée of the chiles and mix with eggs, butter, syrup, vanilla, butter, and nuts. Pour the filling into the crust and bake for another 35 to 40 minutes. Let the torte cool before serving.

BANANA JALAPEÑO DESSERT BREAD
Serves 4 to 6
—

1 cup (2½ dl) flour

2 teaspoons double-action baking powder

1 teaspoon ground nutmeg

½ teaspoon salt

⅔ cup (1½ dl) confectioners' sugar

4½ ounces (125 g) unsalted butter

1 egg, beaten

2 bananas, mashed

2 tablespoons fresh jalapeño chiles, finely chopped

Preheat oven to 350 (175C) degrees.

In a bowl, mix flour, baking powder, nutmeg, and salt. Beat the sugar and butter in the bowl of an electric mixer until fluffy. Add the egg and continue beating until smooth. Add the flour mixture, stirring a little at a time. Then stir in the bananas, chiles, and ½ cup walnuts (optional).

Butter and flour a loaf pan. Fill with batter and bake in oven for 45 to 50 minutes or until knife comes out clean. Let cool on a rack under a kitchen towel.

CHEESECAKE CALIENTE
Makes 20 cookies
—

This is something new to fill the cookie jar. These are cheese cookies rather than cheesecake, but if you double the batch you can make a cheesecake, too. Don't forget to double the time in the oven.

Filling:

1 egg

7 ounces (200 g) cream cheese

3 heaping tablespoons (½ dl) sugar

1 tablespoon fresh lemon juice plus zest, finely chopped

½ teaspoon vanilla

1 pinch salt

3 tablespoons (½ dl) green Anaheim chile flakes or other green chile flakes

Base:

2 tablespoons (25 g) digestive biscuits, ground

2 tablespoons (25 g) gingersnaps, ground

3 tablespoons (40 g) melted butter

Glaze:

3 tablespoons (¹/₂ dl) sour cream

1 tablespoon sugar

1 teaspoon fresh lemon juice

Preheat oven to 300 (150C) degrees.

In a bowl, mix the biscuits and gingersnaps with the butter until smooth. Fill about 20 muffin cups with 1 teaspoon of mixture. Press the base of each cup to flatten.

In the bowl of an electric mixer, combine the ingredients for the filling to make a thick, creamy batter. Fill each cup by using a pastry bag and tube. Bake in oven for 15 minutes. Meanwhile, prepare glaze by combining ingredients in a bowl. Take the cookies out of the oven and pour 1 teaspoon glaze on each one. Bake again for another 5 minutes. Let the cookies cool and then refrigerate before serving.

ANCHO-CHOCOLATE TRUFFLES
Serves 4 to 6
—

The ancho chile has flavors of coffee, cocoa, and dried fruit—all of which complement chocolate. A sensational treat!

6 ounces (175 g) dark chocolate

¹/₄ cup (50 g) unsalted butter, melted

1 egg yolk

Scant ¹/₂ cup (1 dl) fresh or frozen lingonberries

1 egg white

3 tablespoons (¹/₂ dl) castor sugar

2 tablespoons cocoa powder

1 tablespoon ancho chile pepper, ground

Melt the chocolate in a double boiler. Stir the melted butter and the egg yolk into the chocolate and carefully fold in the lingonberries. Meanwhile, whisk the egg white and the sugar together until stiff peaks form.

Carefully fold in the egg white with the chocolate so the batter does not lose too much volume. Refrigerate for at least 1 hour.

Form small truffles by using your hands or a melon scoop. Roll the truffles into a mixture of the cocoa powder and chile pepper, which has been blended together on a plate. Keep in a cool place before serving.

ANCHO-CHOCOLATE BROWNIES
Serves 8
—

4 ounces (120 g) dark chocolate

1 cup (250 g) unsalted butter

2 to 3 dried ancho chiles, soaked in warm water for 3 hours, seeded and puréed

1¼ cups (175 g) wheat flour

1½ teaspoon baking powder

4 eggs

Scant 1¼ cups (250 g) sugar

1 teaspoon vanilla

Preheat oven to 350 (175C) degrees.

Melt the chocolate and butter in a double boiler. Stir in the ancho purée, flour, and baking powder. In the meantime, beat the egg with the sugar until fluffy.

Carefully fold the chocolate mixture into the egg mixture. Spread the batter in a baking pan, 10 x 14 inches (25 x 35 cm) and bake for 30 minutes in the oven. Let cool and glaze.

Glaze:

1 ounce (30 g) dark chocolate

¼ cup (50 g) unsalted butter

¾ cups (150 g) sugar

3 tablespoons (½ dl) milk

Bring all the ingredients to a boil in a saucepan and then reduce heat and let simmer for about a minute while stirring carefully. Let the glaze cool before glazing cake. Wait another 20 minutes before cutting the cake into squares using a sharp knife.

CHOCOLATE PHYLLO NAPOLEON WITH MASCARPONE AND STRAWBERRIES
Serves 4
—

Phyllo dough can be bought ready-made, usually frozen, in most specialty stores.

4 sheets phyllo dough

parchment paper

Brush with sauce:

¼ cup (½ dl) cocoa

3 tablespoons (½ dl) sugar

1 to 2 teaspoons ancho chile pepper, ground

4½ tablespoons water

Filling:

3½ ounces (100 g) mascarpone

*2 ounces (50 g) dark
chocolate, grated*

*2 cups (½ liter) straw-
berries, sliced*

Confectioners' sugar

Preheat oven to 350 (175C) degrees.

In a saucepan, bring the chocolate sauce ingredients to a boil,
remove from heat, and let cool.
Put the parchment paper on a
baking sheet and spread a sheet
of phyllo dough on top. Brush the
sauce on the dough in a thin layer
and then add another sheet.
Brush the sauce on this sheet too,
and continue until all the phyllo
and sauce have been used.

Cut the layered phyllo into 16
pieces. Bake in oven for 10 to 15
minutes. Let cool and then powder with confectioners' sugar.

Mix the mascarpone with the
grated chocolate. Layer mascarpone and chocolate-phyllo pieces
with the strawberries to make a
high "Napoleon cake." This dessert is always appreciated for its
dramatic contrasts in flavor.

Chocolate Phyllo
Napoleon with
Mascarpone and
Strawberries

COFFEE-CHOCOLATE-PASILLA CHILE CRÈME CARAMEL
Serves 4
—

Caramel sauce:

½ cup (1 dl) sugar

7 tablespoons (½ dl) water

Custard:

1 cup (2 dl) cream

1 cup (2 dl) milk

3 tablespoons instant coffee

4 tablespoons grated Ibarra chocolate or 2 tablespoons cocoa

4 tablespoons sugar

2 teaspoons ground pasilla or ground ancho chile pepper

2 large eggs plus 2 egg yolks

Kahlúa liqueur

Preheat oven to 350 (175C) degrees.

Make the caramel sauce first. In a saucepan, boil the sugar with 3 tablespoons (½ dl) of water. Add remaining water and let boil for another minute. Pour the sauce into an ovenproof baking dish or individual ramekins.

Heat the cream and milk in the same saucepan you used for the caramel sauce to add flavor.

Bring to a simmer. Add the coffee, chocolate, sugar, and chile. Simmer for a few more minutes and then remove from heat. Beat the eggs in a bowl and then add them to the heated cream-milk while stirring carefully.

Pour the mixture into the baking dish or the ramekins and place in a water-filled pan. Cover with foil and bake in oven for 30 minutes. Lower heat to 300 (150C) degrees and remove the foil. Bake for another 20 to 25 minutes.

Let the crème caramel cool and refrigerate. Before serving, put the dish or ramekins in some warm water to help loosen custard. Use a knife around the edges and turn upside down onto a plate. Sprinkle a few drops of Kahlúa on custard and enjoy.

IBARRA CHOCOLATE-PECAN SOUFFLÉ
Serves 4
—

Care and precision are key if you want to succeed with a soufflé. In this recipe, make sure the chocolate isn't too warm when mixing it with the egg whites, which must be perfectly cold and clean to achieve stiff peaks. Make all the necessary preparations in the right order so that you don't run short on time. Good luck!

5 ounces (150 g) Ibarra chocolate or other dark chocolate

1 ounce (30 g) unsalted butter

Confectioners' sugar and extra butter

4 egg yolks

½ cup (1 dl) pecans, walnuts, or hazelnuts, roasted and finely chopped

2 teaspoons ground pasilla or ground ancho chile pepper

4 egg whites

4½ tablespoons (70 g) sugar

4 soufflé dishes

Preheat oven to 375 (190C) degrees.

Melt the chocolate and 1 ounce of the butter on low heat in a double boiler. In the meantime, butter the dishes carefully and dust with sugar.

Whisk together the melted chocolate with the egg yolks, nuts, and ground chile. Set aside to cool.

Beat the egg whites until fluffy, adding a little sugar at a time.

Carefully fold the egg whites into the chocolate and fill each dish with the batter.

Bake for 15 minutes in oven. Keep the oven door shut during

baking time. Remove soufflés and powder carefully with confectioners' sugar. Serve immediately.

SPICY CHIPOTLE BREAD STICKS
Makes about 35 breadsticks
—

Spicy breadsticks are great as snacks or as an accompaniment to salad. These are studded with sea salt, but you can also vary the recipe with garlic, rosemary, grated cheese, or chopped nuts.

1 teaspoon active dry yeast

⅔ cup (1½ dl) lukewarm water

1 cup (200 g) unbleached wheat flour

½ cup (50 g) cornmeal

1 teaspoon salt

3 tablespoons (½ dl) olive oil

2 teaspoons chipotle en adobe or chipotle paste

Sea salt

Dissolve the yeast in the water. Let stand for 5 minutes. Add olive oil, ¼ cup of flour, salt, and chipotle and mix to make a smooth batter. Add remaining flour and keep mixing to make a smooth dough. Knead the dough by hand for 15 minutes or with an electric mixer for 5 minutes.

149

Put the dough into a bowl with 1 tablespoon of the olive oil. Turn the dough over to moisten the surface so it will not dry out while rising. Cover the dough with plastic wrap and let rise in the refrigerator for 2 hours.

Preheat oven to 450 (230C) degrees.

Take the dough and place on a well-floured surface. Use a rolling pin to roll out the dough into a square, 18 x 12 inches (45 x 30 cm). Cut into strips, 1/2 to 3/4 inches long (1½ to 2 cm) and place on a baking sheet dusted with corn flour. Let rise for 30 minutes. Brush with water and sprinkle with sea salt. Bake for 7 to 8 minutes in oven. Let cool on a rack.

CORN BRIOCHE MUFFINS
Makes about 20 muffins
—

Corn brioche muffins are excellent to make and freeze for special occasions. Heat them up for breakfast and serve toasted with marmalade. Try adding 1 tablespoon chopped jalapeño or chipotle to the dough!

First step:

1 ounce (approximately 25 g) active dry yeast

²/₃ cup (1½ dl) water, room temperature

¾ cup (100 g) unbleached wheat flour

Second step:

1 egg, beaten

1½ cup (175 g) unbleached wheat flour

Scant ½ cup (50 g) corn flour

1 teaspoon salt

½ teaspoon sugar

3 tablespoons (45 g) unsalted butter in cubes, room temperature

Scant ½ cup (1 dl) fresh corn kernels

4½ tablespoons (1 dl) milk, room temperature

1 egg yolk

First step: Proof the yeast in the water and then add flour, working the dough for 2 to 3 minutes to make it smooth. Scrape the sides and cover with a moist kitchen towel or plastic wrap. Let rise for 1 hour in a warm room.

Second step: Add egg to the dough and mix carefully. Add all the flour, a little at a time, and then add salt and sugar. Use a food processor to mix dough thoroughly for 10 minutes. The dough will stick to the inside of the bowl. Add the butter gradually, working it in, and then add the corn and the milk.

Place the dough in a greased bowl and turn it a couple of times to prevent the surface from drying out while rising. Cover the dough with a moist kitchen towel or plastic wrap and let rise for 2 hours in a warm room. Then let it rise for another hour in the refrigerator, which will make it easier to knead the dough.

The dough can rise in the refrigerator for 8 hours or overnight. Take the dough out of the refrigerator and let sit at room temperature for 2 hours before kneading it.

To shape the bread, knead the dough by pressing the inside of your hand against it and pulling from the edges toward the middle. Turn it over onto a floured surface and shape it into a long loaf. Put flour on your hands, pinch off a piece of dough, and roll it in your hands to make a ball slightly larger than a golf ball. Put each ball into a muffin cup and let them rise for another 2 hours in a warm room. Cover with a moist kitchen towel while rising.

Heat the oven to 400 (200C) degrees. By now the muffins will have doubled in size. Brush them with the egg yolk whisked together with cold water and place them in the middle of the oven for 20 to 25 minutes. Tap your finger against the bottom of a muffin; if there is a hollow sound, they are done. Let them cool on a rack.

WALNUT AND JALAPEÑO COUNTRY-STYLE BREAD

Makes 2 loaves

—

A really tasty bread requires a quality germ and bran flour, proper kneading, and a long time rising in the right temperature. This is one of my favorite breads: Moist, full of nutty wheat flavor, jalapeño bite, and with a beautiful crust. Feel free to use this recipe as a base for other flavors, too.

First step:

Scant ½ cup (1 dl) water

1 teaspoon active dry yeast

Scant 1 cup (125 g) unbleached wheat flour

Second step:

2½ cups (6 dl) water

½ teaspoon active dry yeast

5 cups (650 g) unbleached wheat flour

1½ cups (175 g) whole wheat flour

1 tablespoon salt

1 cup (2½ dl) walnuts, hazelnuts, or pecans

6 fresh jalapeño chiles, seeded and finely chopped, or 4½ tablespoons pickled jalapeño, rinsed and chopped

Walnut and Jalapeño Country-Style Bread

First step: Proof the yeast in the water. Let stand for a minute and then stir with a wooden spoon. Add the flour and mix to make a smooth batter. Continue stirring for another 5 minutes or until the dough is elastic and smooth. Scrape the dough from the sides of the bowl and cover with plastic wrap or a moist kitchen towel. Let the dough rise for 2 to 10 hours in a warm room, or overnight. The longer the dough rises, the more flavor the bread will have. Remove the dough from the refrigerator and let sit at room temperature 2 hours before kneading it.

Second step: Add water and yeast to the bubbling dough and mix until smooth. Add about 1 cup (2 dl) of the flour and all of the salt. Continue mixing and gradually add remaining flour until it becomes difficult to mix with a wooden spoon. Turn the dough onto a floured surface and continue kneading by hand. The dough will be very sticky and hard to handle. Flour your hands and knead the dough by pressing it against the inside of your hand and pulling from the side towards the middle while adding the rest of the flour, a little at a time. Knead the dough for another 15 minutes until it is smooth and elastic. Knead in nuts and jalapeños. Check whether the dough is kneaded enough by pulling it to see if it pulls back at once. If it does, it's ready.

If you have a heavy-duty electric mixer, knead the dough for 6 to 10 minutes, or by hand for 10 to 12 minutes.

Shape the dough into a round ball and turn it around in a bowl with some oil, to prevent the surface from drying out while rising. Cover the dough with a moist kitchen towel and let rise until double in size, 2 to 3 hours in a warm room.

Knead the dough again for 2 to 3 minutes. Let the dough rest under a kitchen towel for 30 minutes before dividing it into two pieces. Knead dough again to get rid of all the air and to reactivate the yeast. Shape the dough into two round loaves of the same size.

Flour a baking sheet and carefully place the loaves on the sheet. Cover with a moist kitchen towel and let rise in a warm room for 1½ to 2 hours.

Heat oven to 450 (230C) degrees. Place the baking sheet in the middle of the oven and spray some water in the oven to create some steam. Shut the oven door to keep the steam in. Do this again after 3 minutes and then bake the loaves for another 20 minutes or until they have turned nicely brown on top. Lower the temperature to 375 (190C) degrees and let the loaves bake for another 20 minutes. Check the bread by tapping your finger on the bottom of each loaf. If there's a hollow sound, the bread is ready.

Let the bread cool on a rack, under a kitchen towel. Wait for at least 20 minutes before serving.

✠ ✠ ✠ ✠ ✠ ✠ ✠

Putting Out the Fire!

When planning a meal, it's important to think about balancing the impact of each flavor.

Strive for a harmony of flavors. Bread, rice, pasta, polenta, and vegetables are examples of foods that absorb the heat of chiles. Dairy products, such as cheese, yogurt, and sour cream, neutralize and cool this heat. What's more, spicy food differs both in heat and taste, depending on the chile—which brings me to the subject of what to drink with your meal. How about chile and wine? The kick from chile won't ruin a good wine. In fact, you'll find chile flavors which parallel the complex flavors of the noble grape. It can be an exciting challenge to find wines which please and satisfy the chile-enhanced palate.

When looking for a wine to go with a chile dish, or when serving any food for that matter, don't let either the wine or the food dominate. Always serve white wine well chilled, as the cool temperature will soothe the heat of the food. However, do not chill below the recommended serving temperature. A distinct, fruity character will balance the intense flavor of the chile. Also, do not combine chile with young, light wines or wines with a lot of tannic acid.

Really hot jalapeño, serrano, or habanero dishes go well with robust, spicy, and fruity Rhône wines from France, or zinfandels from California. A well-chilled Alsace (e.g., Gewurtstraminer, pinot gris, or riesling) is also an excellent choice with its flowery, fruity sweet flavor. A chardonnay with a tropical flavor is suitable with a medium-hot jalapeño dish and a sauvignon blanc or a full-bodied cabernet sauvignon goes well with the hot smoky flavor of the chipotle. A mild ancho with lots of coffee, cocoa, and plum character goes well with a rich pinot noir.

The Muscat grape, known as the mother of all grapes, is used to produce some of the world's finest dessert wines. The Portugese Sétubel and the Australian "liqueur muscat" are strong, sweet wines with a full, fiery, dried fruity flavor that goes well with chile. Marsala speciali—flavored with egg, coffee, and aromas of almond, raisin, and chocolate—is spectacular with chocolate desserts. Let your personal tolerance level for hot flavors decide which wine you will enjoy with your meal.

Beer has always been considered the best accompaniment to hot food. Cold beer with flowery hops and a moderately bitter flavor goes well with the intense heat of chiles. American porter, ale, and dark lager (such as the famous Anchor Brewing and Samuel Adams) are among my favorites. A light Mexican beer (such as Corona, Dos Equis, and the darker Negra Modelo with a slice of lime in the bottle neck) is also to be recommended. Or how about a beer flavored with Serrano chiles such as Rosanna Red Chili Ale? Or maybe a Cave Creek Chili beer from Arizona with the statement, "Lime is for wimps" on the label.

Whatever you do, don't drink water if you think the food is too hot; water will only spread the hot flavor around in your mouth, doubling the heat. On the other hand, perhaps that's just what you want!

Turn the page for some examples of mixed drinks that I enjoy before, during and after, a hot meal.

MALTA CON HUEVOS
Serves 4
—

This is a real energy drink with a dark, sweet flavor and full body. Serve it with hearty sandwiches, chile con carne, or a big juicy steak.

2 eggs

2 tablespoons brown sugar

2 bottles porter, ale, or dark lager

2 teaspoons ground pasilla or ground ancho chile pepper

Use a blender to mix together the eggs, sugar, and porter. Serve immediately in tall glasses with a little ground chile pepper on top. ¡Arriba, abajo, al centro, adentro!

AGUA FRESCA
Serves 4
Agua fresca is a Mexican drink to enjoy with any dish and is made from a variety of fruits. Mango, pineapple, or cantaloupe are great substitutes for watermelon.

Scant ¹/2 cup (1 dl) sugar

1 cup (2¹/2 dl) water

Juice of ¹/2 lemon or 1 lime

¹/2 watermelon, seeded

In a bowl, dissolve the sugar in the water and add the juice from the lemon or lime. Cut the melon into small pieces and put in a blender with the sugar/water mixture. Blend until consistency is smooth.

Stir in crushed ice and refrigerate. Great with a hot meal or just by itself on a hot summer day.

CHILE-LACED HOT CHOCOLATE
Serves 4
—

If you can't find Ibarra chocolate, you can use dark chocolate, sugar, and a cinnamon stick or Valrhona's celaya chocolate flavored with cinnamon.

2¹/2 cups (6 dl) milk

5 ounces (140 g) Ibarra chocolate, grated

1 teaspoon ground pasilla or ground ancho chile pepper

Cognac, rum, or whiskey (optional)

Heat all the ingredients in a saucepan until almost boiling, whisking continuously to give the chocolate a cappuccino-like consistency. Serve in heated mugs and flavor with a drop of cognac, rum, or whiskey.

Index

LIQUID MEASUREMENTS

Cups and Spoons	Liquid Ounces	Approximate Metric Term	Approximate Centiliters	Actual Milliliters
1 tsp	⅙ oz	1 tsp	½ cL	5 mL
1 Tb	½ oz	1 Tb	1½ cL	15 mL
¼ c; 4 Tb	2 oz	½ dL; 4 Tb	6 cL	59 mL
⅓ c; 5 Tb	2⅔ oz	¾ dL; 5 Tb	8 cL	79 mL
½ c	4 oz	1 dL	12 cL	119 mL
⅔ c	5⅓ oz	1½ dL	15 cL	157 mL
¾ c	6 oz	1¾ dL	18 cL	178 mL
1 c	8 oz	¼ L	24 cL	237 mL
1¼ c	10 oz	3 dL	30 cL	296 mL
1⅓ c	10⅔ oz	3¼ dL	33 cL	325 mL
1½ c	12 oz	3½ dL	35 cL	355 mL
1⅔ c	13⅓ oz	3¾ dL	39 cL	385 mL
1¾ c	14 oz	4 dL	41 cL	414 mL
2 c; 1 pt	16 oz	½ L	47 cL	473 mL
2½ c	20 oz	6 dL	60 cL	592 mL
3 c	24 oz	¾ L	70 cL	710 mL
3½ c	28 oz	⅘ L; 8 dL	83 cL	829 mL
4 c; 1 pt	32 oz	1 L	95 cL	946 mL
5 c	40 oz	1 1/4 L	113 cL	1134 mL
6 c; 1½ qt	48 oz	1½ L	142 cL	1420 mL
8 c; 2 pt	64 oz	2 L	190 cL	1893 mL
10 c; 2½ qt	80 oz	2½ L	235 cL	2366 mL
12 c; 3 qt	96 oz	2¾ L	284 cL	2839 mL
4 qt	128 oz	3¾ L	375 cL	3785 mL
5 qt	4¾ L			
6 qt	5½ L (or 6 L)			
8 qt	7½ L (or 8 L)			

Length	Temperatures	Other Conversions
⅛ in = 3 mm	275F = 140C	Ounces to milliliters: multiply ounces by 29.57
¼ in = 6mm	300F = 150C	Quarts to liters: multiply quarts by 0.95
⅓ in = 1 cm	325F = 170C	Milliliters to ounces: multiply millilters by 0.034
½ in = 1.5 cm	350F = 180C	Liters to quarts: multiply liters by 1.057
¾ in = 2 cm	375F = 190C	Ounces to grams: multiply ounces by 28.3
1 in = 2.5 cm	400F = 200C	Grams to ounces: multiply grams by .0353
1½ in = 4 cm	450F = 230C	Pounds to grams: multiply pounds by 453.59
2 in = 5 cm	475F = 240C	Pounds to kilograms: multiply pounds by 0.45
2½ in = 6 cm	500F = 250C	Cups to liters: multiply cups by 0.24
4 in = 10 cm		
8 in = 20 cm		
10 in = 25 cm		

Would you like to read more about chiles?

Here are some of my favorite chile books.

Andrews, Jean. *Red Hot Peppers* (Macmillan 1993).

DeWitt, David. *The Whole Chile Pepper Book* (Little, 1990).

Hazen-Hammond, Susan. *Chile Pepper Fever: Mine's Hotter Than Yours* (Voyageur Press, 1993).

Miller, Mark. *The Great Chile Book* (Ten Speed Press, 1991).

Naj, Amal. *Peppers, A Story of Hot Pursuits* (Knopf, 1992).

I'd like to thank the following people for inspiration and support:

To my family, Cecilia Eriksson and Alicia Borssén, as well as Jenaro Fernández Cosio Baca, Annika Bladh, Jonas Dahl- bäck, Anders Hemming, Berit Erikson, I ka Eriksson, Eduardo Fuss, Lasse Hy Björn Lindberg, Robert Lundin, Raim ström, Robert Reed, Gunilla Sondell, Pɛ ström, *Gourmet* magazine, Sharon A. Tɪ Library at Stockholm University, Eva- Arie de Zanger.

Jonas Borssén